The Shamanic Way of the Bee

"Simon Buxton's unusually wondrous tale, combined with his exquisite use of words, brings radiant life to an ancient shamanic path: the Way of the Bee. Delve into the mystery with Buxton— the story and teachings are brilliant!"

Sandra Ingerman, author of
Soul Retrieval and *Medicine for the Earth*

"As Simon remarks in his fascinating and inspirational book, sometimes we have no choice but to lie still so that we may become a speck in the universe and drink in the nature of the world. I call my soul to be present to witness the power of European shamanism and my friend's journey with the honeybee. Ometeotl."

Elena Avila, MSN, RN, Curandera/Aztec shaman healer
and author of *Woman Who Glows in the Dark*

"Every now and then there is a book that is not only well thought out but well thought of, one that dares to offer ancient wisdom for the modern spirit. Simon Buxton's *The Shamanic Way of the Bee* is such a book. It offers a brilliant and timeless perspective while tantalizing the reader with a splendid, eloquent, and comprehensible presentation. A leading voice in shamanism, Simon Buxton has given us a truly remarkable book, one that is destined to withstand the test of time and lead us farther down an ancient path in contemporary times."

Ken Eagle Feather, author of *A Toltec Path*

The Shamanic Way of the Bee

Ancient Wisdom and Healing Practices of the Bee Masters

Simon Buxton

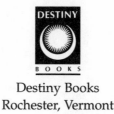

Destiny Books
Rochester, Vermont

Destiny Books
One Park Street
Rochester, Vermont 05767
www.InnerTraditions.com

Destiny Books is a division of Inner Traditions International

Library of Congress Cataloging-in-Publication Data
Buxton, Simon.
  The shamanic way of the bee : ancient wisdom and healing practices of the bee
masters / Simon Buxton.
    p. cm.
  Includes bibliographical references.
  ISBN 0-89281-148-X (hardcover)
  1. Bees—Folklore. 2. Bees—Mythology. 3. Bees—Religious aspects.
4. Shamanism. 5. Healing. I. Title.
  GR752.B44B89 2004
  398'.3699799—dc22

                                        2004012022

Printed and bound in the United States at Lake Book Manufacturing, Inc.

10 9 8 7 6 5 4 3 2 1

Text design and layout by Rachel Goldenberg
This book was typeset in Weiss

To the sweet honeybee, *Apis mellifera.*
To Herr Professor, Opener of the Ways.
To Alice, Rose, Sam, and all the children of today,
wise ancestors of tomorrow.
And of course, for Bid Ben Bid Bont.

Contents

Acknowledgments

I wish to thank Sandra Ingerman for her friendship and support, Dr. Michael Harner for his wise mentoring and encouragement, Professor Stuart Harrop for walking between the worlds with such grace, Ross Heaven for his golden heart and poet's quill, Naomi Lewis for kindling and sharing the hearthfire, Kate Shela for shared high adventures, Ithell Colquoun for the Wisdom Sword, the Sisters Six for parting the trembling veil, the Dreaming Arrows for their forever circle. To the Bee Masters and Mistresses who blazed the trail in very different times, illuminating the way for those who followed in their wake: *le gach beannachtai agus gra.*

Foreword

It is easy to overlook the obvious when we live within a particular culture or country. We who write about inner traditions often turn our gaze to the perfumed East, the wizards of the Amazon, or the witch doctors of Haiti without considering or perhaps even noticing our own native traditions of myth and magic. And yet all the power and majesty is there—or rather, it is *here*—within our Western culture, in our own rolling hills, dark forests, and primal landscapes, in unseen worlds that hide within and behind these "visible faces of spirit."

In this fine and unique book about a European shamanic tradition, Simon Buxton leads us into a hidden world of magic, adventure, and sometimes danger, where the things we take for granted as "normal" and "ordinary" in fact hold arcane knowledge from a reality that humanity has known about, though perhaps only semiconsciously and in half-thoughts, from the beginning of time. This knowledge, this mystery is all around us all of the time; we just need to be shown where to look and need to be given the eyes to see it.

The hidden tradition of bee shamanism provides these eyes. Perhaps the most enigmatic, mysterious, and private of lineages within European shamanism, it traces its history back over thousands of years and has survived the dawn of the industrial age and the introduction of new technologies—yet it remains essentially unknown. Century after century the tradition has stayed hidden and unnoticed right beneath our gaze. Though many of its findings and medicinal tools are now in common use—honey, pollen, propolis, and royal jelly, for example—they are best known as "health foods." Their shamanic origins remain little understood, and the ceremonial use of these substances is known hardly at all. And while acupuncture is now universally regarded as an important therapeutic tool, few people know that it may well have originated from the application of bee stings to the meridians of the body, a medicine that was discovered quite separately from (and possibly well before) the Chinese system.

In *The Shamanic Way of the Bee*, Simon Buxton—now an elder of the tradition of bee shamanism—shares with us his true adventure story of initiation into this ancient order. As with all unusual experiences, his immersion in this new way of being was sometimes terrifying, sometimes exquisitely beautiful, sometimes so strange as to defy rational explanation. Through his honest reporting and the poetry of his words, Simon allows us access to all of his fears as well as the joy of his discovery. In honeyed words the practices of bee shamanism are openly and enthusiastically revealed here for the first time, and the tradition explained as a vital part of our heritage and an intensely practical system of wisdom, spiritual development, and well-being—a tradition that is very much alive, important, and relevant to the lives of modern seekers.

Because of his unique status within the tradition, Simon is able to report from inside the phenomenon in a way that enables us to share his experiences with him, carrying us into the heart of healing practices and techniques of spiritual communion that are among the most ancient and time-tested on this planet.

His journey commences in Vienna and details the beginning of Simon's childhood initiation through his friendship with a mysterious elderly professor of anthropology who (unbeknownst to Simon) is also an Austrian bee shaman.

The meeting is fortunate, not least because at the age of nine Simon is diagnosed with encephalitis, which puts him into a coma and leaves his parents waiting for his inevitable death. It is only through the shamanic intervention of "Herr Professor" that the young boy's life is saved. After this, Simon's training in bee shamanism begins with his introduction to the hive and the healing powers of nature.

Some years later, and apparently quite by accident, he meets another remarkable and charismatic man who seems to have a great deal in common with his teacher from his younger days— including a strange affinity for bees and an understanding of the hive. This man is eventually revealed as the living elder of the Path of Pollen, to which Herr Professor may also have belonged, and becomes his mentor. So begins Simon's formal induction into the mysterious world of bee shamanism.

As Simon's adventure unfolds, he and we, his readers, are enchanted by magic, initiated into specific rites, and led through powerful rituals of personal transformation. Hidden teachings are imparted regarding the symbols of the tradition, the use of bee venom as a means of healing, and the medicinal and ceremonial uses of "the gifts of the hive" as shamanic tools for changing the body as well as the consciousness and spiritual awareness of the user. Some of these secrets may even hold the key to immortality.

As fantastic as all of this sounds, I will vouch for every word of it. I have known Simon Buxton for many years and have had the pleasure and the privilege of teaching with him on occasion. I have also been his student and know him as a fine teacher, an intelligent and ethical man, and a person of complete integrity. He has genuine miracles to impart. This book makes an outstanding contribution to our repertoire of spiritual wisdom, taking us inside a remarkable hidden world of wonders and magic that is going on all around us if only we knew how to see it. Through the music of his worlds and the poetry of his living adventure, Simon makes this possible, something for which, I suspect, we should all be very grateful.

ROSS HEAVEN,
AUTHOR OF *VODOU SHAMAN*

1

Last Night, As I Was Sleeping

Last night, as I was sleeping,
I dreamt—marvelous error!—
that I had a beehive
here inside my heart.
And the golden bees
were making white combs
and sweet honey
from my past mistakes.

ANTONIO MACHADO,
"LAST NIGHT AS I WAS SLEEPING"

There are no clear sounds but the distant, white-noise hum of blood in my ears, a signal that I am still alive. Sometimes there is the sense of a song, but no images come in from the outside world. I am alone here, small and frightened, lost in a snowstorm of white light against the black sky of my eyelids.

I don't know how long I have been here. I am nine years old and the world has been this way for days. Only years later will

I come to know the name we give to this condition: encephalitis, a virus that attacks the brain. For now, names and labels are meaningless. All I know is darkness and stillness.

And then a face appears, one I think I recognize. An old man smiles at me as I drift here in the dreamscape, crying the silent, fearful tears of a small boy standing at the edge of a vast drop into death. "Nothing to fear, little one," he says. The words are spoken in German. He takes my hand. Together we leap into the abyss.

But we never land. I open my eyes and look into his. They are no longer those of a human being. I am looking into eyes comprising countless magnificent hexagonal lenses, each one of them able to see deep into my soul. They are the eyes of a bee, and we are flying.

Effortlessly, we arrive at the other side of the abyss and gently float to Earth. I look into those eyes again, and now they are human. I know them. They are the eyes of a friend.

He smiles at me. *"Kleine Bubbe, alles ist in Ordnung. Habe keine Angst,"* he whispers. "Little one, all is well now. Nothing to fear."

Two days after this dream, I am well enough to eat. A week later, I am out of bed and back to being a life-filled little boy.

I decide, then, to visit my friend Herr Professor after so long away from him. I walk through the woods separating our two isolated houses, past the beehives he keeps in his garden, up to the dark wooden door. Before I can knock, the door opens and Herr Professor smiles down at me.

"Ah, little one," he says. "How lovely to see you. There, I told you there was nothing to fear."

I had met Herr Professor two years before this, when my family moved from the north of England to the forests of Vienna, Austria. His was the only other house within a mile of our property—if you could call it a house. It was more a marriage between a Tyrolean chalet and a jungle hut. It stood in its forest home, shrouded in creeping undergrowth that he cultivated to the minimum so that it remained as wild as possible. He always preferred to be part of his surroundings rather than master of them.

My parents befriended Herr Professor when we moved into our home. Recognizing him as a learned man, they asked if he would teach me German. He was happy to agree, but in the end we studied little of the language. Instead, we had adventures, exploring the wild forest in this strange new territory. Or he would allow me to play his many drums—huge flat drums from Tuva and Lapland and other strange-sounding, faraway places. Sometimes he held me spellbound with stories of his adventures in the jungles of Mexico and Peru, illustrating his talk of jaguars and snakes and dugout canoes, ecstatic rituals and full-moon rites with the curios and objects of power he had brought home: spears and shields, stones and vines, and, most fascinating to me, a shrunken head from a mysterious Amazonian tribe.

We were immediate friends. In the isolation of the woods, I was glad to have someone with whom I could talk and take walks. This wise man shared his knowledge of both the woods and the world, and he revealed the richness of the gifts they contained. Herr Professor had lived in solitude for so long that my youthful exuberance was a joy to him, my company a source of gentle amusement.

Of course, I did not know him then as a professor—though I always referred to him by his title—but as a friend. Later I learned his true identity. He had been a university professor, an extremely well-respected man who had lectured to thousands of students for nearly half a century, and he had traveled the world in search of a personal truth. He had journeyed to the five inhabited continents and the farthest corners of the world. He had lived with indigenous peoples, adopting their simple lifestyles until scientific study had given way to personal belief and immense respect after watching the shamans and wise men and women of these tribes perform their daily miracles that defied the laws of his Western science.

He had brought back these gifts of understanding to his university, and his students had benefited. But he had brought back something else, too: the powers of the shaman. In his respect and admiration for these "wild" men of power, he had worked with them and finally been initiated into the mysteries at the heart of their traditions. In particular, he had learned the secrets of a shamanic path so ancient and secretive that we have largely lost our knowledge of it: a lineage that works with the power of bees to manifest its miracles in the world.

Despite being retired from academic life and in his eighties, he remained as vital and youthful as a man half his age. Instead of seeking prideful recognition as a revered scholar in the circles of academe, he had chosen to reject this false status symbol and become one with nature again, simplifying his life so its natural forces could flow through him and connect him to the world of true power.

That world was all around us. Bears and wild boar moved through the forests.* These were not creatures many people would want to meet close up: their tusks and claws could kill a person if their owner was startled or provoked. My father had told me to be cautious of them—but they loved Herr Professor.

One day while out walking together, I watched mesmerized as a dark shadow shifted into a foraging bear. He looked up and seemed to recognize Herr Professor, and then, to my amazement, he trotted bashfully toward him to have his back patted and neck tickled. As my wariness receded, Herr Professor looked at me and smiled. "Nothing to fear," he said.

Then came the day in my ninth year when I fell ill. As their concern grew, my parents called in the finest local doctors. None of them was able to accurately diagnose my condition, but

---

* Bees, bears, and boars are known within European folk-memory as psychopomps—conductors of souls from this world to the next. Legend has it that a bear would collect the souls of humans in his belly for safekeeping during hibernation. Come spring, he would emerge from his den and eat a laxative plant to release the plug of hair and vegetation that blocked his anus during the winter, allowing the safely held souls to be released. The boar also has distinctive psychopomp attributes: His tusks are shaped like crescent moons and his black face symbolically lies between the dying and resurrected moons, just as three dark moonless nights separate the waxing and waning moon. It is in part based on this observation that the boar is considered a link between this world and the Lands of the Dead.

all of them agreed on the gravity of my illness. They finally gave my parents the heartbreaking news that there was nothing they could do. With sadness and shock, my parents resigned themselves to the impending death of their youngest son.

It was then that Herr Professor had come to call upon his friend—to pay his last respects and say good-bye, or so my parents thought. As I drifted in and out of consciousness, I had the sense of a lifeline being thrown to me. His was no spoken good-bye; it was a gentle song that called me home.

Whenever I would briefly regain consciousness, Herr Professor would be there, smiling at me and whispering something I could not understand as words but that filled my soul with warmth and made me feel safe. He would often rub a piece of wood gently along my neck as he intoned words that seemed to have no meaning but felt immensely powerful and, at the level of my body, beyond the rational mind, made perfect sense to me. I felt myself growing stronger.

And those eyes . . . It may have been my delirium, of course, but whenever I gazed up at Herr Professor, I seemed to be looking into multiple eyes, magnificent eyes, eyes with thousands of lenses that saw right into me. Then I would sleep.

My parents attributed my healing to natural causes, but I had a sense that something more had revitalized me.

Herr Professor and I began to spend more time together after that, and there seemed to be an added depth and a new warmth to our relationship. In every shamanic culture he had visited, the elders believed that a person is called to be a shaman by the spirits in the form of a mysterious illness that suddenly descends on him and takes him to the abyss of death. He is saved only through the intervention of another shaman. Herr Professor had recognized the symptoms of this calling in me.

In the language of a child, he began, slowly and softly, to teach me the ways of power. Between our forest walks and our conversations, I began to develop a deep respect for the knowledge and skills of the shaman and for nature, which he revealed to me as "the visible face of spirit." The alpha and omega of his teachings were within the hive and its inhabitant, the honeybee, and I began to learn the rudiments of beekeeping. I watched— and then copied—Herr Professor's demeanor and behavior toward his hives, and I was stung only rarely, when my jerky movements attracted the bees' attention. While administering a little balm to the stings, Herr Professor would tell me, "Bees, like other animals, respond to the manner of those around them. Move more slowly." As my affinity with the bees began to grow, I started to put drops of honey on my arm to deliberately draw them to me, just as I had been shown. In just a few moments several would land and extend their probosci—their long, grooved tongues used to suck up nectar. Once the honey was gone, the bees would explore the rest of my arm, carefully picking their way along the hairs now starting to grow, while I remained still, fascinated at the sensation of tiny feet upon my skin.

I would have stayed there forever in the cathedral of the forest, learning its sacred teachings and receiving the wisdom of its High Priest, my friend Herr Professor. But it was not to be. Two years after the miracle of my healing, my family left the forests of Vienna and moved to another part of Europe. I wept as I made my way to Herr Professor's house and said good-bye. "Little one, you have a whole world to be part of. Embrace it," he comforted me. "Life is nothing to fear." But I could see in his eyes that he, too, was sad.

He gave me three gifts that day. One of them was a piece of wood that bore a simple yet eloquent carving. I would later learn that this was a *phurba,** a healing stick used in Tibetan shamanism that is used to draw out and absorb negative spiritual intrusions inhabiting the body and causing illness. If, as has been noted, fine architecture is frozen poetry, then shamanic power objects might be described as an act of will, distilled in form and time. It was this simple piece of wood that had brought me back to life when all the medicines and treatments of modern science could not save me—this and Herr Professor's faith in the power of the universe to intervene on my behalf because he wished it so.

I never saw Herr Professor again, but not a day goes by that I do not think of him, and sometimes I weep. He was my friend. Of course I owe him my life, but I also owe him more than my life. It was through our friendship that I first experienced the powers of the shaman. This has driven me to explore further into this tradition so that, in a sense, I may be more like Herr

---

* The earliest phurbas were made from mud. Today they are made from flint, wood, and, most commonly, metal. The phurba corresponds to the World Tree and the world axis, and it is one of the central tools of the Tibetan Bon-Po shaman.

Professor and follow the truths he showed me. If these truths could have such a remarkable, death-defying and life-affirming effect on me, then who else might they help? Perhaps they can save another child, lost and alone in a world of darkness.

Truth, however, is no easy matter. It is complex, strange, and fluid—open to question, a living thing. And yet it is the place where we have to begin, and in the end it is all that remains.

Through my studies, I have come to understand that truth, specifically spiritual truth, can only be defined as that which one knows, without words, to be true. It is silent, and it requires no defense. My challenge in writing this book, then, has been to find the words to express this ineffable wisdom, as well as the truths contained within the shamanic tradition in which I was initiated.

Although nameless in the outer world, the tradition is known by its members as the Path of Pollen, centering as it does on the honeybee and the hive—not merely as a metaphor, but also as a source for an astonishingly rich shamanic knowledge. This book passes on the teachings in the fashion I received them, and often in the context within which they were given. What I present here is a chronicle of specific experiences and observations, reported to the best of my ability—a willful act of ethnography.

Bee shamanism itself, although obscure and hidden, can be located in many different parts of the world—the Americas, Australia, Africa, and elsewhere. The Path of Pollen is part of the rich tapestry of European shamanism, but for historical reasons involving missionization and persecution, it has barely been written about. This may be considered astonishing by some—that an ancient yet sophisticated and unfragmented shamanic tradition has survived into the twenty-first century without coming to the notice of church or state, or, for that matter, anthropology. But there has been neither need nor inclination for my predecessors, colleagues, or companions to put pen to paper regarding their work and their world.

By contrast, there is an abundance of writing on other shamanic traditions, much of it readily available.* There is such richness to this subject that it would be unwise of me to attempt a précis in a few pages. This book details one specific adaptation of shamanism that was developed by the ancient races of the British Isles and Europe. It is a little-known form of Keltic†

---

* I recommend *The Way of the Shaman*, by Dr. Michael Harner, and *Shamanism: Archaic Techniques of Ecstasy*, by Mircea Eliade. The former gives the reader the primary praxis and methodologies of the shaman's path with an exceptionally clear presentation of a weighty subject. The latter is the outstanding scholarly classic on the history of shamanic studies.

† The word Keltic is drawn from the archaic word *keltoi*, which we first see applied to the Celts in Greek and Roman writings. The Greeks and Romans came to use it to mean "strangers" or "barbarians," but it is likely that it derived from a Celtic word meaning "secret" or "hidden." I use the word to refer to those within Celtic culture who were—and are—the keepers of hidden wisdom, who concealed the teachings of their lineages by committing nothing—or very little—to writing, relying instead on the oral tradition to safeguard their knowledge. These people existed and exist within Celtic culture, but their tradition is not identical to that of this broader culture. The term is quite different, therefore, from the word Celtic, which has come to denote the Irish, Scots Gaelic, Old Welsh, and Breton races rather than the holders of arcane knowledge, who were the Kelts.

shamanism that owes its particular expression to the people of these lands, their personalities, their cultures, and the landscapes and geography of their home.

Where powerful, arcane information is being transmitted from one person to another, the oral tradition is usually the safest way of protecting this knowledge from those who might put themselves and others at risk by using it without the protection of full sacred procedure. This book, then, is not another addition to the many tomes exploring or celebrating what the historical Celts may or may not have done, harking back to a time when the world was a very different place. It serves little purpose for modern seekers of truth to invoke the Avalonian mists of yesteryear, if only because those are not the times we live in. Rather, when I use the term Keltic, I use it as a lyrical abstraction; it refers to an attitude and a mood, a state of mind and a poetic sensibility. We cannot all be Celts—for we all, every one of us, have our own rich ancestral roots—but we can all, if we so wish, draw from the deep well that is Keltia.

My initiatory teacher, whom I met as an adult and whom we will meet later in this book, believed strongly in a principle he called "spiritual osmosis," in which proximity to the sacred will itself provide answers. There are no fixed rules, or, rather, the rules and the truths you find will be personal to you. Truth must always be individual, and you will find it from your own experiences and your interpretation of these. By reading this book, you will be drawn into the mystery that is the Path of Pollen and from that will come understanding. I am delighted only that I have been able to bring this powerful, hidden knowledge into the public domain. Reading it is enough; the spiritual osmosis will have its effect to the appropriate degree.

Above all, this is a book about the knowledge, ideas, and experiences that have made up a gateway into a world of my personal spiritual truth. I hope you may also be inspired to cross this threshold and embark on the rich adventure that is the hero's journey, and to discover a truth to sustain you in these times of spiritual uncertainty, but certain opportunity.

2
The Gate of Transition

Ask the wild bee what the druids knew.
OLD ENGLISH ADAGE

He was a beekeeper named Bridge and, as I was to learn, he was something of a legend. He lived simultaneously in the past, the present, and the future, a bridge across, through, and outside the circles of time. He has been described in various ways by those who knew him, but the words that have stayed with me across the years are that he was "a poet with an axe." His thoughts were crystal clear and diamond hard, and yet within him there was room for magic and wonder.

When I first met him, he was, give or take a few months, exactly the same age as Herr Professor had been during my time in Vienna, and like Herr Professor, he stood more erect and moved more briskly than men half his age. His eyes were a clear, twinkling azure, and his smooth, unwrinkled skin looked like burnished copper. He had a magnificent iron-gray crop of hair and eyebrows like caterpillars from the Tree of Knowledge. His voice never weakened or cracked, and he possessed a heart carved of Welsh oak.

More than a decade had passed since my time with Herr Professor and my encounter with death in the Viennese woods, most of them spent in searching—for what? For connection, I suppose, for communion once again with the elemental forces of nature and with the truths that had whispered through the trees. My eyes had been opened all those years ago by Herr Professor's mysterious ability to change destiny and outcomes through the power and will of nature. And so, it seemed, it was the same quest: a passion to understand, to comprehend, to be a part of this world, so different from the one I saw around me every day in the working people with haunted eyes who willingly boarded trains bound for the prisonlike compounds of desks in offices. I had studied philosophy at one of the great institutions of learning and received plaudits for my work, but it had left me hollowed out, for I had found it arid and futile, obtuse and ultimately meaningless—lacking instrumentality, which it seemed to me its teachers craved.

I was part in and part out of that world myself, so I knew something of it—enough, anyway, to know that I never wanted to be trapped within it. I needed no reminding that old certainties were subject to fluidity and transformation, irrespective of what the "authorities" might have us believe. In my youthful, coltish fashion, I was attempting to link a passionate skepticism with the desire for meaning, to find the human key to the inhuman world around me, to connect the individual with the community, the known with the unknown, and to relate the past to

the present and to my own future. But in all of this, I was lost—
a sailing boat without sails or rudder.

My first encounter with the beekeeper was in the spring of
1986 within the grounds of a country house whose land I had
strayed onto on one of my extended walks across the Quantock
Hills in the south of England, the landscape so beloved by
Coleridge and Wordsworth. It was a spring afternoon and I
found myself exploring the extensive, old-fashioned scented
gardens at the back of a property surrounded by farm tracks,
fields, hills, and woods.

I noticed a gate on the farthest wall, a wall of some considerable beauty that had mellowed over time into shades of honey. I
strolled over to it and placed my hand on the latch, leaving it
there for a moment as I took in the Latin inscription that had been
skillfully carved into it: *Hic Habitat Felicitas*—Happiness Dwells
Here. As I pondered whether to proceed uninvited through this
gate, the choice was made for me as I felt the rusty metal latch
begin to move from the other side. I jumped back as the gate
opened and a burly, gnomelike figure—he could not have been
taller than a Shetland pony—stepped forward. With his longish
white hair, a complexion that seemed rarely to have witnessed the
light of day, and a short green felt coat, he could have stepped out
from the pages of a children's fairy tale. This peculiar effect was
further emphasized by his eyes, which were a steady burnt black,
as if borrowed from the gaze of a Russian icon. I noticed that they
would momentarily meet mine and then flicker away, and I realized that this little human was as blind as a mole.

I was uncertain how to respond. Presuming him to be the owner of the property, I weakly and ineffectively remained silent, thinking that I could creep away unnoticed. But he knew I was there, sensing me standing to one side, or perhaps hearing my breathing.

"Have you visited our Eden?" he asked with a gentle familiarity. Flushing with embarrassment, I replied with a stuttering apology that I had been exploring his garden.

The little man smiled at my awkward demeanor and shoved his hand forward to meet mine. "My name is Gwyn, and this is the Gate of Transition," he said matter-of-factly. "It is where the visible is put at the service of the invisible and it divides our world; on this side we operate in one way and on the other side we operate in another." With that he announced that it was time for him to leave, and he strode off toward the house, leaving me openmouthed with amazement. I was utterly bemused by the encounter and could only assume that he had somehow mistaken me for someone else. This false identification I felt gave me the courage to explore further, remembering the blind man's invitation to look beyond. Some time later I was to learn that this man—Gwyn Ei Fyd—had just moments before completed his apprenticeship with the beekeeper—and here I was about to commence my own.*

---

* Gwyn Ei Fyd was Bridge's penultimate apprentice and was considered to be a seer, one who witnesses the world not with the eyes but with the entire body. He considered that his physical blindness assisted him in "seeing" what is invisible to most others, and

I put my hand on the latch once again and the gate swung open to my touch. There was a certain murmur in the air that suddenly grew in force and volume, and, searching for the source, my eyes traveled to the other side of the gateway. There I saw an orchard, sun dappled and carpeted with green grass, which stretched away under ancient apple trees. And there were beehives, perhaps a dozen or more of them, all east facing, each one displaying different colors and markings.

The orchard was alive with bees winnowing the March sunlight with their wings, and there in the midst of them stood a man, hallowed in a mist of bees. He held his space like a magician on a stage who takes handkerchiefs and paper and makes them fly, or like a weaver knitting some strange fabric made from living things. There was something else, too. It was as if he were lit from within, with a sense of love and deep respect that seemed mutual between the man and the bees, and that now made a curtain between us.

He was looking directly at me, smiling through the living veil as if he had been expecting me. I was overtaken by the strangest and most all-pervasive sense of a fate being encountered.

He held me like a mesmerist and I was unsure how to react. Should I move toward him, introduce myself? But the bees . . . it

was a skilled beekeeper, having the ability to detect a queenless or a hungry bee colony by "seeing." He was also a master of the poetics of space, which was outwardly expressed in his talent as a maker of labyrinths, large unicursal paths that he carved out of turf and marked with granite.

had been many years since I had had any contact with a hive. Should I stay where I was and say hello, or would that be somehow rude? Would I be revealing a fear, a weakness?

Cautiously, I stepped forward and opened my mouth to speak, but before a word could form on my lips, a single winged creature darted toward me like a pellet from a catapult. To my utter astonishment, it did not stop. Instead of flying around me or colliding with me, the bee flew through me, or should I say *into* me, for I saw the bee touch my skin and then—vanish! I was rendered immediately dumb, my mind seeking a rational explanation for this disappearing act. Was it the light of the day? Perhaps I was simply not paying attention and it had flown around me at the very last moment. Perhaps, my skittish mind whispered, I now had a bee moving around my body and it would sting me and I would die. Suddenly, I felt a sharp jabbing pain in the palm of my left hand and I let out a yelp. A bee had stung me as I had gripped and released my hands in the tension of the moment. Surely this must have been the bee that had vanished?

The scent from the release of the bee venom in turn agitated other bees, who, reading the chemical signals of their dying companion, came to do battle. I looked up to see the beekeeper watching the scene unfold. I caught his eyes and they were stranger now—a mix of sympathy and interest, kindness and infinite calm.

There was no mistaking the menacing roar: The air was full of angry bees. Once truly roused, I knew that bees were invincible, and sure enough I was stung again, this time on the crown of my head. Despite feeling the sharp prick of the stinger as it entered my flesh, this time I did not move. The lessons I had learned from childhood had stood the test of time.

I saw the beekeeper's eyes again and they were narrower now, really *watching* me. I remained still, although my eyes were weeping involuntarily with the sharp pain on my head. The bee-keeper nodded very slightly. Yes? Was that a yes? Yes to what? And then, suddenly, the bees were gone. I disengaged from his eyes, looked down at my palm, and felt the top of my head, which pulsed in rhythm with my racing heart. I looked at the space around me, which should have been filled with bees, but it was still. The bees had gone back to their foraging, their honey making, their hives.

The beekeeper beckoned me over to where he stood, beside one of the hives, now humming gently with a kittenish purr. "You were stung," he said simply in a voice that was a song, a gentle, melodic Welsh lilt. It was a statement more than a question, delivered with interest more than concern.

"Yes," I said, "here on my hand and head."

At that, he took my hand and something remarkable happened: The pain (it was really more of an irritation) immediately subsided.

"You were stung directly in the center of the *dream wheel*," he said, referring to the tiny wound on my head. "It is one of your *interior stars* and is the part of us that comes into the world first, the part where our first senses of the world reside, and the place where we attempt to make sense of our reality. It sees the world before we do. It is one of your magic circles." His voice moved with a certain bardic weirdness that sounded both euphonious and enraptured. Despite not fully understanding his words, they seemed to lead me, almost hypnotically, into an uncanny zone, somewhere between the land of heart's desire and a wasteland created by history.

By way of introduction, I told the beekeeper about my previous experiences with bees through my meetings with Herr Professor, and for the first time in my life, I told the story of my healing, and the gifts that my learned friend of the forest had given me. The beekeeper had many questions regarding Herr Professor and would on occasion nod affirmingly when I spoke of certain matters, such as my memory of the healing and some of the few facts I knew of the man. I finished by explaining that this was over a decade ago, and that I hadn't been near a hive since.

"Then you must come back to the hives and learn more," he said cordially, "as it seems the bees have a liking for you!" He laughed as I inadvertently touched the top of my head. "You might say you had a calling in that respect," he added.

And so, very casually, I began to return to the country house of Monks Bench, to the walled garden, to the orchard, to the hives, and to Bridge the beekeeper, to learn more about his craft and the nature of bees.

From the very first encounter I was aware that Bridge possessed an unusual intensity and an interior quality that radiated his communion with the honeybee. When working with the hives, there was something priestly about his behavior, as if he were undertaking a ritual that could be witnessed only by himself and his bees, a ritual that would result in contact with the transcendental. This was rooted not in the fantastic or the fanatical, but rather in a simple, grace-filled communion with nature.

I would watch him as he would go to a hive, subdue it, open it, and draw out the brood-combs, bringing them over in a carrying rack with the bees clustering in thousands all about them. A scent diffuser was brought into play, and, as the combs of several hives were sprayed with lavender gathered from the orchard, the soothing fragrance would wash over us.

Bridge and I would move around the orchard, inspecting the flora and fauna of his citadel. Built into the deep walls were aged, arched recesses known as bee garths, which used to hold old-fashioned bee skeps—hives—humming with life. Herbaceous borders edged with arabis and aubretia, clumps of crocuses and snowdrops, were within easy reach of the hives, as well as bergamot, forget-me-not, hyssop, sage, mignonette, Michaelmas daisies, lavender, mallow, rosemary, and red broom that appeared like butterflies of raw flesh. Hawthorn, sycamore, and lime trees were grown for their high yield of nectar, and a small well, fed by an underground spring, produced cool, sweet water that the water-bearing bees collected for mixing food for the children of the hive.

At times, a dark cloud would drift across the sun and the foraging bees would become chilled. In the cold, bees' wings become paralyzed, and they would drop to the ground unable to rise or even crawl. When Bridge observed such casualties I would watch him—just as I had watched Herr Professor—gently pick up and cup a cold little body in his hands and breathe warm air upon it. Every time I witnessed this miracle, I felt the same wonder and delight in watching a lifeless bee revived, just as I did as a child. After a shuddering convulsion the bee would get on its legs and dust itself, first brushing the antennae with the forelegs and then raising up the abdomen and dusting it vigorously with long sweeps of the hind-leg brushes. The bee would then jerk its triangular head from side to side and, having made sure that the last atom of dust had been removed, it would fly off like an arrow.

"Bees are skilled astronomers," Bridge announced to me one day in an exaggerated, theatrical manner. "They can predict rain. And they were created from rays of light. Were you aware that they suck their young, completely formed, from flowers? Or that honey is created in the air when the stars rise and a rainbow rests upon our Earth? And did you know that any woman who is a virgin can pass through a swarm of bees without getting stung and at exactly midnight on Christmas Eve, the bees hum hymns to celebrate the birth of Christ? If a bee flies into your house, it means a visitor is coming. Stolen bees will not thrive, but die. Our medieval scholars taught that bees were born from the dead bodies of cows and calves. These, young lad, are just some of the superstitions that have arisen regarding our winged friends, but in truth any single bee can do the impossible in order to maintain the wholeness of the hive."

Bridge went on to detail facts that were as remarkable, if not more so, than the superstitions: how a wounded, starving, or plundered hive could actually moan in agony; that the bee can grow old quickly, and then grow young again—sterile bees can lay eggs in times of crisis and the senile can rejuvenate glands that have atrophied. Bridge also asserted that beekeepers rarely become ill and rarely if ever contract cancer or other terminal diseases. I considered this a very bold claim, but later I researched it and largely found it to be true.*

There was certainly little doubt of Bridge's own well-being, and he ran off a list of historical figures who had benefited from their relationship to the honeybee and the hive. "Pythagorus, who maintained a diet involving a great deal of honey, lived to the age of ninety. One of his disciples, Appolonius, dined on a diet of milk and honey and lived to be 113. Pliny the Elder records that there were 124 centenarians living in the region

---

* Two examples of my research into this assertion: D. C. Jarvis, M.D., of Vermont, writes, "I spent two years checking the observation that beekeepers do not have cancer. Charles Mraz, a beekeeper in Vermont, helped me in this study. Together we were unable to find a single case of cancer in beekeepers or learn of one who had died of the disease. In his international search for cancer among beekeepers, Dr. B. Beck discovered one case. That was a man who died of skin cancer in Hawaii." (Jarvis 1985) Dr. W. Schweisheimer stated, "A strange observation some 20 years ago had been made by the Berlin Cancer Institute. Its scientists and doctors had never seen a bee keeper who was suffering from cancer." (Schweisheimer 1967)

between the Apennine Mountains and the Po River—not bad for such a tiny domain. Honey has always been part of the diet of the native Britons; indeed, the original name for Britain translated as 'the isle of honey.' Did you know that Plutarch observed, 'These Britons only begin to grow old at 120 years of age'! Well, my own teacher left the world just a few feet from where you are standing, but he achieved only his one hundredth year, so he was still a youngster in Plutarch's book! Beekeepers—like the finest of wines—are better when aged."

Through these first meetings with the beekeeper, I was reminded of the trinity of the hive—the three types of bee described by Herr Professor that make the honeybee family complete: The *drones* are the bucks of the community and swagger around, dandified and handsome and largely contemptuous of any honest work. Hatched in the early summer to provide suitors for the young princesses, they lead an idle life, leaving the hive only during the warmest part of the day. The drone possesses no sting, but his wings are powerful and his senses acute, with a delicate sense of smell and amazing powers of vision.

The workload of the hive falls upon the *workers*, the female bees who produce the wax, which is secreted by their bodies; build the cells; fill them with honey; feed and nurse both the queen and the worker larvae; collect the pollen, nectar, and propolis (a curious antibacterial resin manufactured by the bees from plants and trees); defend the hive from enemies; and perform a thousand other duties. They are the ones who bring about the harmonious prosperity of the colony.

The *queen* is truly a queen in the ancient tradition. She is longer than her daughters, more slender than her sturdy sons, and mated with her own brother. In all her long lifetime—which exceeds, by perhaps six or eight times, that of even the longest-lived of her children—she sees no other bees except her sons and daughters. In her solitary person she carries the destiny of all, and she is as a goddess whose life is devoted to selfless service within the dim light of the golden city.

Within these three types are the young ones—the bee children in their new velvet suits, brought out by the bee nurses, sitting in the sun and waving their legs enthusiastically to the swift, unheeding bee traffic that passes over them; and the guards—warrior women workers—conspicuous as if arrayed with swords and helmets, who wait at their observation posts near the entrance, challenging every comer.

Without the honeybee, Bridge remarked, our Earth would bear a very different appearance: "There would be nuts and grass perhaps, but practically all our fruit and flowers would be absent. To survive, the bee has accomplished miracles and has tackled and overcome problem after problem. At times, she has accomplished the seemingly impossible."

We continued to meet through the summer months and into the early autumn. Bridge reacquainted me with the knowledge of how to work with bees, to understand them, and to reap the fruits of the hive. I enjoyed our meetings and felt that I was learning something—a skill that was useful to me, and a form of meditation almost, as we worked together in the quiet of the orchard. I watched and learned. Often we worked silently, but when Bridge did speak, it was with such poetry and presence that I would remember well his observations. "The commonest things in nature are always the most beautiful. To link rarity with loveliness is but the human infraction of the wider theme." I also began to see what sort of man Bridge was. He was flinty and blunt with a remorseless logic, but his words never came cheap; if he offered instruction, he exacted an expectation as to how these teachings would be honored and applied. He was a man of quiet epiphanies and solemn enunciations.

I never left empty-handed from a meeting with Bridge. He rarely slept, making an encounter with him equally exhausting and exhilarating. It was not unusual for us to work from sunup to sundown, followed by chess through the evening. Bridge was a patient opponent, and on occasion he would play with his back to the board, calling out moves. This cerebral duel was accompanied by the massive and intense music of Puccini, Strauss, Verdi, and Wagner, his love of which he traced back to the womb, for while pregnant his mother listened to nothing but grand opera on her gramophone player. After my slaughter on the board, he would rise to spend time in the apiary and I would be allowed to "take counsel with my pillow" for a few hours, before the cycle of work started once again.

I had seldom, if ever, liked anybody so much or so quickly— a feeling that remains undiminished after more than seventeen years. He possessed a single-minded humility, a passion to unearth truth. He was a master physician of the soul in his insights and a profound sage in his conclusions. It wasn't simply what he had to say; it was also his presence—a kind of charm that was part subtle intelligence and part a kind of innocence, not of the naive kind but of the type one likes to suppose saints, holy people, and prophets have. He also gave off the authentic, potent whiff of otherworldly power.

I began to see that thinking of him as a beekeeper was actually quite the wrong expression for this man. He did far more than simply keep bees; somehow, I felt that he was *of* them. Certainly the bees knew and respected him. He was, I was to learn, a Bee Master—an artist working with living form.

But the term *Bee Master* may be easily misunderstood, for he was not the master of the bees in the sense that he used them in any way. If anything, he would say he was their servant, or perhaps their co-worker. He was a master of the art of beekeeping and had an understanding of the behavior of bees that was quite astonishing. He was able to talk with them, to commune with the hive, assessing the unique qualities of the bees and handling them accordingly. They responded to him in a way I have not seen before or since. They would often sit as a small ball upon his left shoulder, with Bridge whispering and singing to them all the while, and a sweet bee song was their response, their lullaby return. On one occasion a swarm landed on his head. There must have been some ten thousand bees. Very slowly, he moved to the doorway of an empty hive and lay down in front of it with his head low. The bees then walked into the hive. On another occasion, we came across a swarm of bees in a local woodland,

THE GATE OF TRANSITION

but had no means of carrying it back to the house. He stood directly beneath it and got me to vigorously shake the branch upon which the swarm had landed, so that the bees fell on him, at which point we walked home and deposited the swarm into a hive. He was, as it were, a chameleon with the bees, his colors ever shifting, effortlessly changing to become the hive.

As we walked around the orchard, which Bridge moved within as a *temenos** inspecting the hives and the plants, I discovered that there was a certain formality to the fashion in which he talked of the art of beekeeping. These talks always commenced with the same four words: *"The Bee Master knows."* This expression, delivered with ritual solemnity, became a signal to me that a teaching session was about to begin and that Bridge was about to impart a "Knowledge Lecture." It was akin to a bomb warning, sending me into a frenzied state of cerebral typing—for to get Bridge to repeat a lecture was almost impossible. *"Vestigia nulla retrorsum,"* he would say in his beloved Latin. "Never retrace your steps."

It was his responsibility to deliver each lecture with flawless clarity and accuracy; it was mine to record them in the same way

---

* The term *temenos* is a transliteration of an ancient Greek word meaning "a safe and protected precinct surrounding a temple." Because the temenos was traditionally the property of a god (or, more commonly, a goddess, such as the groves of Artemis or Diana), within its protected space people were afforded temporary sanctuary from the secular world. In the modern world, a temenos has come to mean a protected physical and emotional space in which the transforming work of healing takes place through learning and teaching.

and then to reflect upon them in quiet meditation. This eidetic approach was a talent forced from me out of necessity.

Over time, I would come to see that these lectures, taken together, made up a honeycomb of essays pointing to the truth—a truth that requires no defense.

I would also discover that it was remarkable just how much one could recall given the correct circumstances. The mind must be still and have the space to quietly review and replay the events and teachings of the day. I became skilled in what amounted to rewinding certain events and watching them as if they were a film. I would then take notes while the film was being played, gradually filling notebooks and building up a practical philosophy based on the teachings I received. Bridge had himself been taught in this fashion, and this commitment of oral teachings to memory, for recitation, had been considered a priority by his teacher, as it was now, in turn, by him. Bridge considered training in memory to be as important a quality as improvisation and creativity, which he maintained were essential for deepening into the craft of the bee.

His first lecture to me was brief and precise: *"The Bee Master knows* that no one species of animal has inspired so many people in so many ways as the humble honeybee. No creature has had more literature devoted to it; a continuous honey flow, from Aristotle and Virgil down to our present day. For thousands of years, men and women have worked with the bee with varying degrees of success, and during this long period we have come to treat this small creature with considerable respect, so much so that the bee is often used to represent purity, integrity, industry, and a host of other virtues.

"They have been on the earth since the Cenozoic period, which is some fifty-five million years ago. And if we look at images from the civilizations of Old Europe, we discover that next to serpents, bees are the creatures most often depicted. They have certain things in common: Both live in small, dark places, both carry venom, and both issue forth from the hole at certain seasons of the year. But whereas serpents might be depicted as symbols of either good or evil, bees were almost always regarded as beneficent. Bees offer us the most beautiful example of community that we shall ever find; they have much to teach us in this regard. When nature has work to be done, she creates a genius to do it: the humble honeybee, our most ancient ally.

"*The Bee Master knows* the bee as the most remarkable of creatures, a social alchemist and truly nature's most astonishing being," he reflected before displaying his discreet passion for language and linguistics. "It has at all times and places been the symbol of life—life as immortality. In the Celtic language, the Cornish *beu*, the Irish *beo*, and the Welsh *byw* can all be translated as 'alive' or 'living.' The Greek word *bios* should also be mentioned. So the bee stands for—and is a manifestation of—the fundamental verb 'to be.' 'I am, thou art, he is' it declares as it goes humming by.

"If we look to myth, the bee is the ritual creature of a host of lordly ones. To anyone capable of suspending for a moment the cavortings of the rational mind, of accepting myth for what it is—not a story or a lie or a corruption of the facts, but the very essence of truth—it should need no great inward effort to access their significance." His eyes bore into me, testing to see if I had yet understood. Then he spoke again, very slowly: "It is a matter, merely, of listening."

He would never deliberately excite the ear, but I nevertheless found myself listening very deeply when he spoke, and without consciously knowing it, I would find that he had taken me to a very strange place—a zone of the soul. He held an unusual combination of visceral energy on the one hand and mercurial thought processes on the other, but he tempered this with a certain measured gravity, a certain detachment that allowed him to change almost alchemically, his metal altering in the crucible of his imagination.

Bridge had traveled widely with his teacher and witnessed the work of Bee Masters across the globe. He witnessed—and participated in—the work of the Australian Aborigines, who would wait at a water hole for bees to come and collect water. They would then use a special weed that exudes a sticky gum to flick a piece of feather fluff onto the back of a bee. This would weigh down the bee and it could be easily followed through the forest to the tree where the wild hive was located, and then the Aborigines would gather the wild honey. He also traveled to the Kayapo people in the Brazilian Amazon basin to work with the bee shamans, who had great skills in identifying different stingless bees and in finding their nests. The bees there would always leave behind honey "for Bep-kororoti, the great bee shaman who was taken into the sky in a flash of lightning." Over time, I heard many of his adventures, eventually becoming a participant in them.

It was nine months on and Bridge began to hint at something that lay behind his beekeeping, a group of bee practitioners whom he called members of a bee *cultus*. I was deeply intrigued.

"We are simple beekeepers," Bridge said, laughing, taking in my wide-eyed expression. "But as well as that, we are the holders of an immense knowledge that has been passed to us from one generation to the next." I asked him if he was suggesting that all beekeepers across the land—and around the world, for that matter—were members of this mysterious cultus.

"All those who keep bees are not *necessarily* members of our tradition. Whether they belong to us directly or not," he continued, "most beekeepers feel themselves connected by a sense of fraternity. We are all linked strangers. Most know nothing of the existence of the bee cultus and merely involve themselves in the mystery without question, and often without awareness that they are tapping into a source of grace and power, reflected in simple terms as great good health and a life of balance.

"The teachings contained within this tradition have been handed down so faithfully that it has never been in danger of extinction. The bee cultus was not created, but rather summoned, and the citadel of the tradition is a fortress that can never be taken. To the uninitiated, the cultus—like the city of the bees itself—is hidden, veiled. Nothing is known of its inner

councils, of the debates and decisions, of the governors and offi-
cers, of the supervisors who allot the tasks, of the regeneration
that occurs and the training that is offered." I was unclear if
Bridge was now referring to the beehive or to the beekeeping
tradition. Perhaps he was referring to both.

Bridge suggested that the bee cultus was ancient, arising
from the time of the first human partnership and interaction
with other living beings. This was a time before agriculture and
the use of animals for human benefit, a time when truly natural
living and mutual cooperation between the land and its creatures
was not only an unquestioned fact of life, but also an accepted
and unspoken necessity for survival. The times of persecution, of
witch hunts and trials, the separation of humans from the land, the
rise of agriculture, industrialization, the dawn of the machines—
all had contributed to force the lineage into the hive, metaphori-
cally, as the perfect place of invisibility.

"You have seen the paintings upon the hives, have you not,
lad?" he said, referring to the images that were carefully executed on and around each of Bridge's hives—pictures of animals,
glyphs, and unfamiliar shapes and symbols.

"*The Bee Master knows* these are our modern petroglyphs—our
'cave paintings,' which connect us back to the earliest members
of our cultus. Archaeologists have not understood that the cave
paintings, as our hive paintings, were not executed as art. Why
were these masterpieces that drew gasps of envy from Picasso
hidden in deep, dark caverns, sometimes in passages so narrow
that only a single person could crawl to see them? Simple: The

walls of the caves were known to be membranes, beyond which lay the realm of wise teachers. The spirit animals and the artist-shaman drew the animals through the membrane and then fixed them onto the surface. The handprints on these walls and the marks of fingers in soft clay indicate moments when our ances-tors reached out to the spirits. When we draw on our hives today, this is this principle we are executing."

Bridge continued, "When people become aware that some-thing is stirring within them, they will usually find a member of the cultus to teach them, allowing them to step into an intimate alliance. And then there are those who have been singled out to one of us older ones." I wondered if he was thinking of the day we first met and of the bee stings I had received. Had this been a signal for him? I distinctly recalled the strange look in his eyes, as if he was watching what the bees were doing, waiting to see if they would accept me.

"Your way has been paved for you by the law of spiritual gravitation. You arrived here on the principal that 'your own will come to you.' It is the force of the cultus itself that has exerted polar magnetism upon us both, and thus we find ourselves in each other's company. The element of chance was entirely absent in our meeting."

3

The Small Branch
of the Great Tree

I have seen the past and it works.

BID BEN BID BONT

The end of the year falls exactly at the beginning of the first stroke of midnight on December 31, and the new year begins as the last stroke ends. But what happens in between?

Bridge put this question to me when we met on the last day of December. I know now that the Bee Master wanted to discover what I knew of the times when the veil between the spiritual and material worlds is at its thinnest—the betwixt and between times so beloved by the Kelts. During these betwixt and between times, we are really nowhere, lost in a place that is neither here nor there, but everywhere at once. Nowhere. Now here.

In answer to Bridge's question, I told him a story I had heard as a child that had stayed with me over the years. A correspondent for the BBC World Service was describing the ceremonies of an African tribal people at the end of their lunar cycle. At a given moment, the chanting and drumming ceased as the gods and deities invisibly withdrew from the world and we poor human souls were left alone for an instant, a lifetime, a forever-moment caught up in a heartbeat, to fend for ourselves. I have often wondered what it might mean—that lost moment—to us of the modern world. Most likely it would go unnoticed by many because we have no rituals pointing out such things to us. For just a few moments, absolute silence reigned in Africa as the gods withdrew. Then the drums broke out again in triumph as the spirits invisibly returned, cradling the new year in their arms.

The reason I had recalled the story was that the reporter, a modern Western man, had added that although he did not expect his listeners to believe him, he would vouch that during the few moments of sacred silence, his tape recorder had completely stopped working. "The betwixt and between time, Bridge?" I asked.

"A good little tale," he affirmed, "and a tale I want you to tell the bees, for they will understand it."

Bridge had recently asked me to start speaking my key realizations to the hives, to begin the lifelong habit of talking to them. Indeed, I was to learn that "telling the bees" is one of the key practices within the bee tradition. So is "asking the bees," as indicated by the old adage "Ask the wild bee what the druids knew," or, as I would amend it in my mind whenever I was given the chance to question Bridge, "Ask the wild druid what the bees knew"! (The word *druid*, used here, refers to a woman or man of exceptional spiritual knowledge.)

These two practices—asking and telling the bees—are clearly linked. But precisely what do we tell them and why, and what do we ask them and for what reason? I would come to learn the answers in due time.

"What we call the betwixt and between times are those moments when we are able to commune most eloquently with what lies just beyond the periphery of vision and consciousness," the Bee Master continued. He reminded me that in meditation that involves working with the breath, there is usually a ritual pause between the outgoing and the incoming breath. "Between one breath and the next, between one lifetime and the next, something waits for a moment. These are the moments in which to act—to initiate new ideas, new relationships, and, dear Twig, to initiate new people."

He had begun calling me Twig several weeks before, with no explanation, after he had inquired if I might be interested in moving more deeply into the work, and received my answer: Yes.

I asked him why he had started to call me by this rather peculiar name. He replied, gravely, that it was a name the bees had given him to pass on to me and that its meaning was my "fruit to pick"—one of his favorite expressions, implying that he was going to give me no further assistance on the matter. In fact, if Bridge ever considered that one of my many questions did not deserve a reply, or felt I was being simple, he would often amend this expression to a curt "Low-hanging fruit, Twig, low-hanging fruit"—meaning, "Easy to get at; work it out yourself"—and on occasion he would edit this down further still, silently mouthing the word *fruit* while arching his eyebrows and ushering me away. Bridge possessed the skill of saying much in few words.

Frustrating though this was, I came to see that not answering a direct question explicitly sets up an inner friction in the questioner. As a result, one question inevitably leads to another, and the answers that come are never conclusions. It was rare for Bridge ever to answer a conclusive yes or no to a question. To him, life was far richer than that.

What he did tell me about my name was fascinating, however, and it offered me further insight into Bridge himself and the tradition of which he was a part. "In the words of Shakespeare's Caesar, it is your 'name to conjure with,' your conjuring name, your magical motto. My teacher gave names to his apprentices, too, and his teacher before him. Or, more correctly, the bees gave the names and the teachers merely relayed them. The full name my teacher passed on to me was, in his native tongue, Bid Ben Bid Bont, which is from the great *Mabinogion** and translates as 'Who would be a leader, must be a bridge.' And so I was named Bridge by my teacher.

"The bees told me that you would be the last of my

---

* The *Mabinogion* is one of the great treasure troves of our Western spiritual heritage. It is a beautiful, colorful piece of Welsh literature that gives way to magical imagery and dramatic narrative. If approached from a shamanic point of view, it reveals much about the spiritual practices of the Kelts. The earliest copy of the complete *Mabinogion* is *The Red Book of Hergest* (circa 1400). An earlier manuscript called *The White Book of Rhydderch* (circa 1325) is considered incomplete, but is still worthy of serious study.

charges—and a bloody relief that was to hear!" he said with a laugh. "You would be, they said, 'the small branch of the great tree.' In my estimation, that makes you a twig, and so you are Twig: The Small Branch of the Great Tree."

It was New Year's Eve, which was the reason for his question about the moment of infinity between the old year and the new. The veiled moon was just tilting over the treetops when we went out to the orchard; in the dim spectral moonlight, it looked double its actual size. It felt as if the evening was stretching itself and the day's muscle had finally relaxed. We seemed to be standing in the midst of a great down with bee dwellings stretching eerily into the darkness. The hives had been recast into mounds by quilted layers of snow, and ice sealed the waters within the ancient well. From every hive there came a dim, deep murmur of dreaming bees. The Bee Master lit his lantern and held it close to the entrance of the oldest of the hives. In his other hand, he held an open jar with a little honey smeared in its base. He began to chant, a quiet, deep, beelike drone. In answer to his call, twenty or thirty bees emerged from their hive and entered quietly into the jar, which he quickly capped. We went back inside to the red glow of the hearth, Bridge, myself, and the bees, and we drew thick velvet curtains against the night.

Bridge disappeared for a moment into a side room and returned with a strange medieval-looking instrument that I recognized from my childhood days with Herr Professor as a bee smoker—a cylindrical firebox, compact enough to be held easily in one hand, with a small bellows attached to its side. When working with the hives, the firebox was usually packed with chips of rotten wood, dung, dried grass, autumn leaves, or pine needles, all of which make excellent smoker fuel; these were then lit and kept smoldering by squeezing the bellows, creating a plume of smoke that was emitted from the hole out of the top of the firebox. This instrument is used to puff thick, cool smoke into the hives, which calms the bees. On detecting the smoke, they forget about tending their home and instead fill themselves with honey; memories are stirred of forest fires and an intention to escape the flames with survival-full stomachs. Sweetly satiated, they become far more docile. Furthermore, when their bodies are filled with honey, it is difficult for the bees to bend themselves into a stinging posture.

The bee shaman, however, as well as using the smoker in this fashion, was also versed in the smoker's secondary function. I watched, as still as a moth on a branch, as Bridge lit the smoker and worked it with the skill of an artificer now wedded to his tools. After a few silent moments working the bellows, he beckoned me over and sent a series of dense puffs of smoke up, down, and across my body. It was not burning wood or dung or crisp leaves that I smelled now, but rather a sweet, honeyed aroma that I knew must be from the hive but could not identify. It was only later I learned this was propolis,* a curious, magical

---

* Mixed with the propolis was giant puffball fungus (*Calvatia gigantea*), which produces a mild, calming effect when burned and inhaled. The name Bridge had for this fungus was Puck-fists, plainly named after the merry spirit Puck, a well-known figure within

substance that had been used by the bee shamans in their work for as long as time itself.

It felt luxurious to have this gushing fountain of warm smoke poured over me. Having dowsed my body, Bridge drew the bellows close to my ears and allowed the warmth to pour into them and into me, coursing and wafting through my mind like a honeyed breeze.* It was delicious and intoxicating, a ceremonial cleansing of great potency and beauty. But in preparation for what?

"Right, lad, you're all done," said the master of the smoke. "Sit down in one of those chairs." I felt drunk with purity, unable to do anything but obey.

The pair of chairs sat opposite each other—*exactly* opposite each other—perhaps three feet apart. They were clearly antique,

---

British faery lore. While working, Bridge would often burn herbs and resins, always ones that were indigenous to Britain and northern Europe. He was critical of those who drew on plants from foreign climates, as he was also about ingesting foreign psychotropic plants, due to their symbiotic evolution with the people of the land.

Among those he used included Scotch pine resin, inula, verbena, mugwort, mistletoe (*Viscum album*), and hops (*Humulus lupulus*—or, more specifically, the delicate yellow powder, lupuli, that falls out of the small lymph nodes on the inside of the flowers). Human hair was burned on rare occasion. But above all, he would always burn propolis, a substance seldom if ever mentioned in writing as a resin for burning. It is a waxy resin produced by bees, dark brown and viscous, and when burned it produces a warm, balsamlike, honey fragrance.

* This action of blowing smoke into the ears was quite deliberate and was undertaken to assist me in being able to "hear true." It is a practice found within various shamanic cultures for the same end. See, for example, the story "El Secreto" within *Los Cuentos de los Abuelos*. (Parra and Hernando 1997).

seventeenth-century oak, I guessed, but what distinguished them from other chairs I had seen from that period were their remarkable carvings. At the very place where the small of the back would fit, a carving protruded like a clenched fist: It was a human male face, immersed in a foliage of oak leaves with branches bearing fruit sprouting from his mouth, eyes, and ears. This was the Green Man, a pagan symbol, though ironically found primarily in Christian places of worship—in tiny churches and great minsters, hidden in corners and emblazoned on bosses. The Green Man is a primal and powerful image of renewal and the continual rebirth of nature, which was brought into the churches originally to attract the people of the land—the *pagani*. To my eyes, this carving made the chairs look exceptionally uncomfortable, and I resigned myself to sitting in discomfort for the rest of the evening. However, lowering myself into the chair as instructed, I was surprised to find exactly the opposite: The Green Man aligned almost perfectly with the small of my back and even offered me support. Whatever else the evening held, at least it would not be spent in the abject suffering I had envisioned.

Once I was seated, Bridge came up to me with a bottle of dark liquid and two glasses, carrying the bottle as a butler might bear a priceless old wine. The cork came out with a ringing, jubilant report and a pale, straw-colored liquid foamed into the glasses like champagne. It stilled at once and the Bee Master held it up to the light. "Mead—a drink brewed from honey and older than the wheel, introduced to me by my teacher as 'druid fluid'!" he said. Then, to my surprise and delight, he

broke out into verse and simultaneously performed a rapid and
lively jig.

> *The juice of bees, not Bacchus, here behold,*
> *Which British Bards were wont to quaff of old;*
> *The berries of the grape with Furies swell,*
> *But in the honeycomb the Graces dwell.*

"Made a decade after you came into the world, Twig, and the
finest year for mead across the country for many a year. The history of mead is as long, rich, and captivating as the beverage
itself. It is the drink of our ancestors, the most ancient of alco-
holic elixirs known to humans, though, sadly, few people have
tasted it.

"This is a special brew, known as a metheglin or, in my
tongue, *medclyglin*—medicine. The old Greeks called it ambrosia
or nectar, and it was considered the drink of the gods, descend-
ing from the heavens as dew before being gathered in by the
bees. It was known to have magical and sacred properties, and,
if made as an act of power and communion with the hive, it will
prolong life and bestow health, strength, virility, creative powers, and—as you can well tell by being in my company—great
wit and poetry! We Kelts know of a river of mead running
through paradise, and even you Anglo-Kelts used to hold up
mead as the bestower of immortality, poetry, and knowledge.
In fact, the mythology of mead exists in our culture today,
unnoticed by most. The very term *honeymoon* comes from the

ancient tradition of giving bridal couples a moon's worth of mead, which was enough to ensure a fruitful union between the two. In the old days, the payment to the mead maker was often inflated, depending on the promptness and gender of the first-born child, which would inevitably come right along!"

Tentatively, I sipped the magical liquor offered to me, not knowing what to expect of this honeymoon drink. The effects were immediate. It tasted of orchards, sandalwood, cedar, and innocence, and some wild mystery beneath the deep potency of the drink. I heard myself sigh, and I relaxed as the alcohol gently flowed into my bloodstream. Bridge filled my glass again, but he drank no more himself, and the thought came to me that a most important occasion must have warranted its appearance, for Bridge was no casual drinker and had sipped it with the intensity of a sacrament.

I was already transported, and, through the mildest intoxication, I watched as Bridge raised the glass above his head and dedicated the drink to the Queen. A casual observer might have seen this as an innocent toast to the head of the British royal family. To those who knew, however, it was a salutation to she who is the center of the hive.

Bridge sat down in the chair opposite me. As he did so, it was as if the night changed and a deep solemnity choked the air out of the place. The claustrophobia of the moment caught me, and I was stilled by it, becoming as a butterfly pinned. Bridge began to speak.

"*The Bee Master knows* that upon this path, the Path of Pollen, there is information and methodology that has been held in trust for millennia, used publicly yet discreetly, when needed for healing, and used by our companions and forebears within this lineage to deepen their communion with the hidden universe.

"On this evening I wish to share with you one of the great secrets of the tradition. It concerns the bee sting. We know it as the Sacramental Venom, or the Secret Fire, a powerful and mystical substance with the ability to transmute illness into well-being alchemically. We have unlocked its application and it has become both an art and a science that has been developed and refined over generations.

"Hippocrates, the father of medicine, was an initiate of the usage of Sacramental Venom, which he called *arcanum*, 'sacred secret.' One of the earliest of the Egyptian papyrus scrolls—the Smith Papyrus, dating back over three thousand years—suggests that its usage was already a refined healing and initiatory methodology by then, and with each generation the refining of the work has continued. We who hold the deeper communion with the hive are the original acupuncturists, holders of an autochthonous system of healing, using the bee sting the way the acupuncturist's needle is used today.

"To this day in China, you will find that a few—a very few—of the older acupuncturists dip their needles in the solar drops of bee venom before inserting these needles into the patient's body. These ancient ones are connected, perhaps by one remove or more, to our lineage. The ley lines, power lines, channels, meridians of the body have been known to the Keepers of Bee Wisdom for thousands of years as passages that connect certain energetic points, allowing energy to circulate throughout the body. The blood and life essences travel through this system of pathways, which connect a multitude of points on the body's exterior and interior. Some of these are points of major energy concentration, which can be adjusted, encouraged, or even rerouted. This not only creates balance and healing, but also, when stimulated by the Sacramental Venom, allows the initiate to enter into the worlds that exist outside of time and space, the place where our ancestors teach us. This teaching is the Magnum Opus, the Great Work, of this tradition."

My mind was working overtime through the effects of the liquor, the moment, and the way the moonlight had conspired to add its solemnity to these revelations. Bridge was saying that ancient societies had found a way not just to heal and balance themselves, but also to give them a route to the gods, through the bee sting. My mind was reeling, but my curiosity carried me beyond questions. I stayed silent.

"True," he continued, "the Path of Pollen has its dangers, for before there is birth there is labor—if honey, then also sting. But at its completion, it confers upon those who attain it extraordinary control over physical conditions. These include the ability to transmute matter, to heal all diseases, and to pro-long the span of human incarnation. The Path of Pollen is our yoga, our means of union and communion with the incredible hidden universe and this beautiful blue-green jewel that is our Earth."

The Knowledge Lecture was complete and I knew there would be no more talking, though I was now bursting with questions. If I had heard him correctly, Bridge had implied—no, more than implied; he had actually *stated*—that the special use of the bee sting and the powers it conferred could change physical matter, cure *all* sickness, and allow the recipient to become, if not immortal, then certainly able to increase his life span beyond the normally accepted limits.

This was not the time for questions, however. Something was about to happen, I knew it beyond doubt. But what? I had never seen Bridge like this before. It was as if he was preparing to deliver a bitter blow to me. Perhaps he would ask me to leave and never return, the final secret having been revealed. I even considered for a moment in the darkness and the heat of the liquor that he would now have to kill me.

Finally, he continued. "I am sharing this with you on this eve because you and I have now reached a crossroads in our work together. You have a choice of roads you may walk. You may step back the way you came and find an open road before you. Or you may step sideways onto a different path, one with fewer obstacles perhaps—one worth considering, my boy! Straight ahead, there is a place of struggle and challenge. This is where I am standing, waiting for you."

His voice deepened, with a sobriety that was at one with the dark. "I wish to formally invite you to join us. If you accept, this will involve receiving and enduring initiation by Sacramental Venom and other tests and blessings beyond this.

47

I wish to invite you to be initiated into—and remembered onto—the Path of Pollen, the Forest Way, the Brotherhood and Sisterhood of the Sacred Hive. I wish to invite you, Twig"—and here he paused for what felt like minutes—"to become my spiritual son."

The night hung heavy, and the air itself seemed to take an inbreath. Nothing moved. It is difficult to explain how I felt at the moment of this invitation. It is not that I do not remember the feeling; it is rather that no single word exists to describe it. I recall that I cried a little, overwhelmed perhaps by a sense of homecoming, as if I knew this place but had forgotten it or had turned away from it and was now being welcomed back by a father who had forgiven me. Though he would never have admitted it, I think Bridge was moved and relieved by my reaction, too. I mouthed the word *yes*, and Bridge stepped quietly toward me. We hugged each other for a brief moment and then he stepped away. *As befits a Kelt*, I thought. Almost immediately, it was back to the business at hand.

"Before we can begin the ceremony, I need you to undertake what is something of a secret within this business of the gods. We know it as the Theater of Ambiguous Behavior."

Just an instant before, I had been moved beyond words, able to make only the simplest of responses to the most wonderful and gracious invitation I had ever received. It was amusing how quickly this mood had passed and I was back to my puzzled, questioning self. "Ambiguous behavior?" I asked. "What do you mean, Bridge? Why?"

He replied, "To begin your transition into the encounter that lies ahead, you must very deliberately undertake actions and thoughts that are doubtful in meaning—doubtful not to me but to yourself, behavior that is to yourself quite indefinite. By doing this, a room will be built between two worlds, where your normal, ordinary state of being will no longer be able to operate, and yet a new state and awareness will not have been conferred upon you. Let us say it is the betwixt and between period, the action of bridging the worlds, if you will."

He smiled ruefully. "Commence when you are ready. It is not a performance, so there is no need for performance pressure; simply deepen into a period of ambiguity and taste the liberty that this simple action brings." At that, Bridge got up and left the room.

It was not much comfort to be told there was no pressure, for I still had hardly any idea of what was expected of me and, moreover, I had to assume that if I did not enter into the state of ambiguity that Bridge had asked for, whatever was meant to follow would not. I closed my eyes and took a few deep breaths, making every effort not to plan my actions or make any decisions about what I might do, as whatever I was supposed to achieve clearly had to be done spontaneously and with no forethought.

Self-consciously at first, I began to crawl on all fours around the room, sniffing table legs like a dog. As I warmed to the task, it began to amuse me to act in such an illogical and irrational fashion. I started to laugh, deep from my belly, and then I leapt up, spinning like a Catherine wheel, dancing like a marionette on invisible strings, then throwing myself to the floor, all inhibition gone, jerking as if in a fit, rolling and gamboling like a child. I was in the space between worlds of which Bridge had spoken, playing the part of the fool in the Theater of Ambiguous Behavior.

And then I felt Bridge's hand on my shoulder. When he had entered the room again, or what I had been doing at the time, I had no idea. Gently, he sat me down again upon the Green Man chair. Not a word was spoken. As I caught my breath, he silently began to trace honey over my forehead in the shape of an eight on its side, all the time intoning in Gaelic, *Tá na ródannaí meala ag na beach in ins gach aird den sliab* ("The bees have honey roads in every cardinal direction from the mountain"), repeating it again and again while sprinkling pollen over my head. Next, he picked up what resembled a small, flat frying pan made of shining copper and quietly spoke to me of what was he was doing, wanting me to learn as well as experience. "This is our drum, Twig. Those who say that our ancestors in these lands did not use a drum in the old traditions have simply been looking in the wrong places."*

He began to beat upon the metal drum with two sticks held together in his right hand, in a regular rhythm. This technique, I was to learn, is known as *tanging:* hitting a piece of metal in such a way that bees respond to the sound and may be easily sub-

---

* To date, no archaeological evidence has been found of drums having been used by our British ancestors for religio-magical work, even within archaeological digs that in all probability would turn up such ceremonial tools, such as peat bog excavations. Since having been introduced to the *tanging quoit*, however, I have seen several examples of this instrument within museum collections, with descriptions as diverse as cooking implements and children's toys.

dued. Tanging is dismissed as superstition by modern beekeepers, but seen through shamanic eyes, it has exactly the same
function as the shaman's drum when played in a certain monotonous beat of four to seven strikes a second. It puts the shaman
into what is known as a Shamanic State of Consciousness, and it
is in this state that the bee shaman does his work. Recent studies* have shown that shamanic drumming produces changes in
the central nervous system and facilitates the production of
brain waves in the alpha and theta ranges related to creativity,
vivid imagery, and states of ecstasy. Indeed, shamanic drumming
can positively affect well-being and the immune response. The
repetitive sound of the drum is the channel through which
shamans travel to other worlds via the shamanic "flight of
ecstasy"—a term that might have been especially coined for the
bee shaman! In Siberia, the drum is known as the shaman's horse;
in the Upper Amazon, it is the spirit canoe in which the shaman
sails to the invisible land. The bee shaman knows this tool as the
quoit and its sound as tanging.[†]

Bridge explained a further reason for the tanging at this early
stage in the ceremony: "Imagine we get a number of old-fashioned
pendulum-type grandfather clocks. Let us hang them on a wall

---

* The work of Dr. Sandra Harner and Dr. Warren Tryon in particular. (Harner and
Tryon 1995).

† If we look at Virgil's didactic poem *Georgics*, it can be seen that he was familiar with
the practice of tanging, which he referred to as the "jangle cymbals of Great Cybele."
(Virgil 1983)

and arrange their pendulums so that they will be beating out of phase with one another. In a day or two, we would discover that all the pendulums would be beating in phase, as if locked together. The larger the number of clocks, the more stable they will be as a unit and the more difficult to disturb, and if one clock becomes wayward, it will be brought back into line very quickly. So, Twig, the tanging will begin to bring you into the same rhythm as those others who walk the Path of Pollen and thus assist in giving you access to the hive."

Bridge began to change his chant to the one he used when tending the hives: a low vibration punctuated with occasional whistles and distinctive clicks. I looked up at him and watched as he controlled his vocalizations deliberately, moving first the upper lip, then the lower, then both together, all the time breathing in a circular manner, in through the nostrils and out through the mouth.

The strange sound filled the room until it became something akin to the hum of the entire hive. The phrase "Ask the wild bee what the druids knew" flashed through my mind and the thought occurred that this was not just humming. Rather, it was the wisdom of ages that the bee shamans had whispered into the hive over centuries, and it was being spoken aloud now by this man chanting in the language of the bees. Some form of information was being conducted directly to my brain. I had become a conduit for this knowledge, yet I knew not what electricity compelled it to me in such a way. No distinct words were discernible within the sound itself, yet at some level my body just *knew* the precious secrets that were being imparted to it and my mind was filling up. Images, poetry, snapshots of human history, scenes from worlds to come flew across my mind in snippets of awareness, like clouds across the moon. The tanging and the chanting continued for some time—perhaps thirty minutes, perhaps an hour.

I felt my body getting warmer and my heart starting to race. The room darkened around me until only the eyes of the Bee Master were still visible. They seemed enlarged and darkened, changed. It was as if I had seen those eyes before, a long, long time ago, though I could not remember where.

I struggled to concentrate, to hold on to my rational mind. I wanted to watch, to question, to record what was happening, to analyze its effect, to understand its method. But it was no good. My body felt stunned and paralyzed and my mind was hitting overload. I was being swamped with sensory information and could feel myself falling backward into some other world of chaos and dreams. Upon his invitation, I had ventured into the dark forest that Bridge inhabited, filled with basilisks and shadows, and I knew now that there was only one way to traverse: straight ahead.

The tanging stopped, but the silence that replaced it was busy with tones and movements of sound. The jar with the bees was opened. Bridge reached into it and brought out a single honeybee. Holding it by its thorax, he brought it toward me, and I was stung on the side of my neck. As tears streamed down my wincing face, two more bees were brought out from the jar, and the other side of my neck and then the top of my head—my dream wheel—were penetrated, receiving the Sacramental Venom. A fourth bee was removed and gently held by the Bee Master. Slowly, he moved the bee closer to the midline of my face, directly between my eyebrows, while the deep harmonic sound of the humming became increasingly resonant and persistent.

I continued to focus on his eyes, which had darkened further. Then, all at once, I remembered. His eyes were those I had glimpsed in the healing dreams of a dying child. Suddenly, I *knew* that my childhood experience with Herr Professor had been an omen, a precognition of this moment, and that all my experiences had led me to this point. I had been called by the bees from the very beginning. As this thought crossed my mind, Bridge reached me and held the bee on the area between my eyes. I felt a dull sting and passed out.

It all began with vibration and a slow dance of golden lights. I was floating upon a sea of electricity, dancing, moving though thick curtains of incredibly beautiful flames that did not burn but seemed instead to cleanse me. I moved in and out of differing levels of consciousness, and I began to make out shapes of human beings, of women.

I gathered that I was sitting, surrounded by six women whom I knew were bees . . . or was it six bees whom I knew to be women? I was naked, and I felt like a baby—trusting them as they began to move forward and lick me, with the tongues not of women but of bees, stretching out and then withdrawing,

sweeping forward and backward. With every lick I was changing, being massaged by their tongues into a deeper world. It
seemed that days and nights came and went, connected by rivers
of honey. I heard distant words—"changing man, changing
man"—and I looked up into Bridge's eyes, the huge compound
eyes of a bee. His lips made strange beelike sounds, which
became wind, then a long screeching whistle, as a torrent of
faces and lines rushed past me.

Everything was falling and simultaneously gushing forward
at an incredible speed, becoming landscapes, pebbles, glaciered
mountains streaked with black ice, spectral rocky cliffs, and
oceans of fermenting honey, an endless production of colors,
rhythms, and forms. More lines flashed before me, crossing like
rivers meeting, endless bifurcations, glyphs, and swollen symbols that copulated in front of me. Language was destroyed,
leaving only intonements and vibrations; there was nothing left
for me to hang on to.

I wanted to retch. I was going to retch. I could feel it: sickness rising. I tried to leap up and stumbled, vomiting, snapping
myself back to full consciousness in one violent purge. Thank
God it was over. I wanted to get away as quickly as possible, to
make sense of it all and recover. It was pitch-black and I could
see nothing. I felt as if I had been involved in a great fire or
earthquake; all that remained intact of me was what was essential to life. And then the emptiness within me, the hole that I
had become, started to fill. With what exactly, I had no idea, but
I clung to it like a thirsty man offered water after a drought.

The sound of humming was quieter now, replaced by a gentle murmuring, and the room around me seemed unfamiliar once again; it was not the room I had been sitting in. Indeed, it was unlike any room that I had been in before. It was so small I could hardly move, and it even smelled different. I presumed that upon passing out Bridge had moved me to another room. Barely had this thought occurred to me when I lost consciousness once more.

The sun, slanting diagonally through the long, narrow entrance to the hive, showed it was well past noon. I took a moment to pull myself together and then I looked around the room, trying to orient myself in this new environment. Hundreds and hundreds of hexagonal wax cells surrounded me in the most exquisite detail. The back wall of every cell faced in one direction and interlocked with another, which faced the opposite way. All their open ends tipped upward ever so slightly, each one of them holding what I knew with mounting horror to be the most precious of freight: nectar, the very soul of flowers. Each cell had been molded into being by the tongues and feet of bees, each flake of wax licked and trampled into place as it emerged from the abdomen of the bee.

A part of me knew that I was within the hive itself, and I was terrified. I knew for certain that I would be detected and stung to death, an alien intruder swarmed by giant bees with stings as vast and deadly as a saber. I looked around in frozen panic, anticipating the moment and dreading its arrival. Sheltered in cells, larvae surrounded me, the growing young on which the colony's future depended. To the side and just above me, a rainbow of cells arched up and over, pixels of pollen grains suspended in its arc, within reach of the nurse bees, who would use them to tend the fattening brood.

I was at the very heart of the hive, the nursery, its most sensitive and protected space, where there were eggs, larvae, and unhatched brood in varying stages of growth. It was a wonder I was not already dead. And then I knew why.

It is hard to say what horrified and repulsed me more: the fact that I was here at all and the certainty that I would be killed in the most brutal and terrifying way I could imagine, or this new realization that now swept through me. The reason I had not been killed was that I was no alien intruder; I was myself *Apis mellifera*, a male drone, surrounded by forty thousand female workers and, somewhere, our queen, our regent.

I do not know how long my terror lasted. But I felt it recede as my own humanity, my sense of what it means to be a human being, began to fade, to ebb, and I became one with this new domain and the knowledge of my part, my purpose here. I was no longer human but a member of a completely different genus. I had a duty to perform, like all of us here within this cathedral. Time, continuous and unbroken, lost its linear movement, and days and nights moved in and out of one another. Perhaps the whole experience lasted only minutes, but outside of ordinary reality, where there are no clocks, an entire lifetime passed.

I heard a rustle behind me and I knew—I utterly and simply *knew*—what was happening: The new queen was about to make her one and only royal voyage out of the hive. She would do this with a single purpose in mind: to mate.

For the drones, this was our ultimate moment, the culmination of all we had lived for. Since birth we had hung around the hive, doing very little other than feast on honey and pollen, tolerated by the female workers, who diligently continued to go about their tasks. What the others did not know was that once this encounter with the queen was consummated, we would be forcefully ejected from the hive—or stung to death if we refused to leave—for our work would be completed and we would have no further function in this place. Our duty done, we would end our lives in cold and hunger.

The virgin queen had been fed well but she had yet to feel the glow of sunshine, and now she was readying herself for the hazard of flight. She approached the edge of the hive entrance and we followed her, inspecting everything in her path with eyes that see both fore and aft, protecting our regent to ensure that her sacred purpose would be fulfilled.

She spread her wings and rose, noticing every small detail that marked the outside of her citadel. She gained altitude, describing wider and wider circles, surveying the site until its every feature became familiar to her. We, her loyal drones, were on the wing, too, observing the timid movements of our virgin queen. Our humming was all consuming, and it soon attracted her attention. She enlarged the circles of her flight and passed over us, inspecting, enticing, urging us to follow, and suddenly we were in full pursuit.

I felt so agile, so free, an impetuous bee child who dared to look upon the queen, who dared to ask for more. I wanted her more than I have ever wanted anything. I was driven by this fire in my belly, driven by the need to mate, willing to fight and die for the privilege of coupling, merging, blending with the queen and impregnating her with the gift of my own seed and my life. I was the strongest, the bravest, the fastest there, and I deserved this.

I flew toward her, willing to destroy any who blocked my way. I was primal, urgent, brutal, lost. And suddenly I was with her. I knew that my ecstasy would be followed by my death but I did not care. This was what I was born for, to fight, to prove myself, to be the best, to leave this world but to carry on in the children I would leave behind, born of royal blood. I locked myself to the queen and in blind, raging passion, I delivered myself to her.

Even as I died—my abdomen exploding in pain-ravished ecstasy—I was reborn. I awakened, breaking through into human form. I was gasping for air, choking, heaving, drenched in cold sweat, and gulping down oxygen as if I had narrowly escaped death by drowning or asphyxiation, unable to inhale fast enough to satisfy the craving of my lungs. And then I began to cry, howling as if I were an abandoned baby, newly delivered into an alien world—a cruel moment of individuation from the connectedness of the one organism that had become my home, my heart, my hive.

Bridge gathered me to him and gripped me hard. "Remember who you are! Remember who you are!" he barked, shaking my arms. "You are Twig," he said, still insistently but more gently now, as a flicker of recognition played across my face. "You are Twig," he said again. "The Twig is the Small Branch of the Great Tree that is the Path of Pollen. You have been welcomed into the hive, as I welcome you back into human arms."

4

The Path of Pollen

Once meek, and in a perilous path,
The just man kept his course along
The vale of death.
Roses are planted where thorns grow,
And on the barren heath
Sing the honey bees.

WILLIAM BLAKE,
"THE MARRIAGE OF HEAVEN AND HELL"

I was in a very bad way, slipping ceaselessly and seemingly without control from one world to the next, hitting the uncertain and ever fluctuating boundaries of psychosis. My only conscious memory from this period was a waking nightmare during which I imagined that I had disturbed a hornets' nest and was defenseless as thousands of them attacked me. A legion of stingers were embedded in my face; hundreds of small barbs endowed with a malignant life of their own quivered and twisted into my skin. And yes, there was pain—upward, downward, in every corner of my world.

The Bee Master eventually placed me in what appeared to be an oversized, six-sided dog basket and threw a blanket over the top of it. I curled up tight, instinct telling me that the chamber offered a safe holding, and for a moment at least, I felt the dark shadows of madness begin to diffuse and dissipate. Gradually I fell backward into a dreamless slumber that was to last many days and nights. A scrap of verse by Dylan Thomas rose up as I slipped precariously down into the arms of Morpheus: "I followed sleep who kissed me in the brain . . . I fled the earth and naked, climbed the weather . . ."

The experience of being inducted onto the Path of Pollen—and thus into the hive itself—had utterly rocked the foundations of my identity. When I would rouse from the numb wilderness of sleep, I wondered if I could ever reconcile my old world to that which I now knew. The experience of my initiation would create a peculiar prism through which I would peer on my old life from this point on, and, in time, this new way of seeing the world would become a personal manifesto. I had been blown off the expected course of my life and was moving around new orbits and new suns.

But for now, as I lay curled within the hexagonal wicker womb, despite the turmoil that the experience had induced, I yearned to awaken within the hive and merge again with the hive mind. My estranged and caged spirit grieved its isolation from the hive, and the monotony of this aching grief collected around me like a toxic smog. At times I would be awakened by my body violently trembling, my emotions moving between a devastating sadness and an uncontrollable ecstasy, accompanied by wave upon wave of searing heat that irritated my skin where the bee stings had been planted on my body. I would scratch at my skin until I felt blood replace sweat at my fingertips.

Eventually, I arrived at a semicomatose visionary state during which colored circles of citrine, russet, and mauve surged up before my eyes, revolving concentrically in a ceaseless, seasick rhythm. An insistent harmonic buzzing of countless bees made a hive within my skull. My body jerked involuntarily, as if being tugged by invisible cords from my belly, and I knew that these cords were connected to the hives and their inhabitants, calling to me, beckoning, pulling, coaxing, seducing. Large, shining black snakes would uncoil in the darkness and the hair on my head would turn into tangled serpents that lashed me with their tails. After a period of this delirium I would pass away into sporadic, fathomless sleep to the sound of my own wheezing breath. Even in slumber I carried myself like a gun, cocked and alert, ready for assault; my teeth would grind, my jaw clench.

Hour after hour, as night followed nightmare, this exhausting pattern continued. Hardly knowing where I was and no longer sure who I was, my world darkening and the shadows increasing, I finally felt the relief of the Bee Master's hand upon my head. My body slackened and relaxed beneath the soothing balm of his touch, and where I had formerly sunk in the clutches of the shadow realm, I was now liberated to a vision that touched each of my senses. I was within the forest in Vienna and inside the forest was a clearing and inside the clearing was a cabin and inside the cabin was Herr Professor and inside Herr

Professor was the hive and inside the hive was the child. And as the child, I drifted into a lullaby of rest.

Occasionally I would smell the traces of honey that had been dabbed on my forehead, and this faint scent would rouse me to emerge from my miniature temenos. In the half-light I would discover a jug of cool springwater from the orchard that had been left for me, together with a small mountain of fresh pollen. I would drink and eat both before crawling back into the safety of my hazel and willow cell.

A pattern of behavior began to emerge of rising in half-light from sleep and eating and drinking what had been left for me—water and pollen alone for some days, occasionally supplemented with honey in its comb and a little milk. More often than not, though, I was greeted by the simplicity of water and pollen. Satiated, I would then slide back into my vessel and dream—dream myself into what I might be, out of what I had been, for what I was now felt like a fossil in stone.

And then one evening—was it dusk or dawn?—the melodic, calming voice of the Bee Master arrived, imparting what, even in my delicate and confused state, I knew had been ever given to the newly initiated. I invoked all my ability to remember his words, just as I was being re-membered upon the path as I drifted between the worlds. The first words from the Bee Master were in the form of a precise brief: "*The Bee Master knows* bee pollen as the Golden Coins and knows that it must be treated as such—a gift from nature of enormous value, to be treated with utmost reverence. When you take your next meal of bee pollen, allow the grains to dissolve on your tongue and make careful note of your experience."

On the next foray from my woven cell I did as instructed and partook of the Golden Coins, imbibing slowly and with deliberation. As the pollen began to dissolve, I distinctly experienced all five major tastes: the sweetness of honey, the spiciness of ginger, the taste of sea salt, the sourness of yogurt, and the bitterness of hops.

Perhaps a day and a night passed before the Bee Master returned, continuing his Knowledge Lecture without missing a beat: *"The Bee Master knows* that through imbibing the Golden Coins, you will have experienced all five major tastes, in specific layers. This in itself attests to pollen's comprehensive effect from an energy perspective, for each taste exerts specific physiological properties.

"The Bee Master knows that pollen is the finest remedy in all existence to nourish and supplement; indeed, it is one of the most complete and unique foods in all of nature. Our bees seek out only the highest-quality pollen, which we use for deficiency conditions and as a preventive medicine. It is the great rejuvenating agent of the world, and is considered to be an elixir of longevity. Our ancestors knew it as ambrosia, and indeed it has always been seen as fit for the gods. The Golden Coins are a miracle food; it is our caviar, our life-giving dust. And because it plays an important role in improving alertness, relieving brain fatigue, improving memory, and increasing capacity for intense concentration, this treasure house of regeneration is your primary diet at present."

As Bridge spoke, a memory from my teenage years rose up of the great athlete Muhammad Ali remarking that he was helped to "float like a butterfly, sting like a bee" by taking bee pollen while defending his heavyweight titles. Bridge went on to state categorically that life can be sustained on bee pollen and water alone and that without pollen, the bee is unable to manufacture venom.

At the time of my next meal, I carefully inspected the small grains that seemed to shine with every hue of the color spectrum, and reflected upon the labor of its collection—gathered from untold thousands of wildflowers, herbs, bushes, and trees by bees who often carried their own weight in pollen back to the hive.

But the Knowledge Lecture was not yet complete. Bridge continued: "Those upon the Path of Pollen have always recognized the beautiful synergy that exists between flower and bee in the making of pollen. In fact, no other botanical in the world is produced in this way. When we consider the application of pollen as a remedy, we can easily see how it was considered to be the true ambrosia, for even the most cursory glance at pollen's actions would suggest that it is nature's answer to virtually every known malady. It has the widest variety of effects and uses of any herb. There is not a single organ, system, or tissue that is unaffected by its influence. Its tropism is global; it is *the* life source; and it offers us a path to the center. It is honored as such.

"In addition to pollen containing more chemical constituents than most other botanicals do—twenty-two in all, the number of letters within the original Hebrew alphabet—there is an as yet unknown and unrecognized ingredient that plays a vital role in pollen's total curative effects. Listen well, Twig: The flower is the *lover* of the bee and he comes to her lusty and pollen-coated. She receives him as a bride with open arms; it is a rich and fragrant lovemaking. What the bee profits from the most is that it derives its sustenance from the very parts of the plant that are pervaded by the plant's sexual energy. The bee sucks and collects this nourishment, pollen and nectar—sucks and collects from the parts of the plant that are steeped in sexual power, its reproductive organs—and thus the bee brings this sexual power from the visible face of spirit into the hive. We know this power as vitamin P. Vitamin P is the *vita*—Latin for life—of Pan; it is vitamin Pan."

He spoke these two words—*vitamin Pan*—with such force that my body momentarily shuddered in response. They were also the two words that completed his talk, and I was left reflecting on how Pan—the horned stag god of Europe—could be connected to honey, pollen, bees, and sexual power. The Knowledge Lecture was complete, and Bridge—if he was even in the room—had become as silent as a shadow. I recapitulated the lecture several times, word for word, until I knew that it was fully anchored in my body. Exhaustion then enfolded me and I was drawn down deep once more into sleep.

The ever-present twilight of my enclosed monastic life within the hermit's cell continued. Time went uncounted. And then a voice from a distant land came whispering through the reeds of my home. It was not Bridge's voice, but as with the timbre of the Bee Master, it was a voice of clear and certain authority. It was also perhaps the most unusual voice I had ever heard, for it expressed itself as much in shapes, sighs, modulations, and murmurs as in words. It was the voice of a woman.

"I
do not
believe in
God because I've
never seen him. If he
wanted me to believe in him,
then surely he would come and speak
with me. He would come in through my door
saying, 'Here I am!' But if God is the hive and
the honeybee, and pollen and nectar and sun and moon,
then I believe in her and I believe in her at every moment, and my
life is a prayer and a celebration and a communion with the eyes
and through the ears. I honor her by living spontaneously,
as a woman who opens her eyes and truly sees, and
I call her the hive and the honeybee and pollen
and sun and moon, and I love her
without thinking of her, and
I think of her by seeing
and hearing, and
I am with
her,
I."*

---

* This was the Bee Mistress's interpretation of "O Guardador de Rebhanhos," by the Portuguese poet Fernando Pessoa. (Pessoa 1973)

The voice continued:

"'Thus I can understand how a flower and a bee might slowly become, either simultaneously or one after the other in the most perfect manner, by the continued preservation of all the individuals that presented slight derivations of structure, mutually favorable to each other.' These, Initiate, are the words of Charles Darwin, who touched on the fringe of a great truth—namely, that embodied in the life and work of our most ancient ally is exquisite mathematical precision; exact geometry is applied to the uniform construction of the diaphanous hexagonal cells, arranged, as you have witnessed, in perfect order."

And then a Knowledge Lecture began from this new voice, delivered not in the style of the Bee Master, which was akin to hearing one of the few inspired academics from my alma mater. Rather, this was a prose poem, half-whispered through the reeds. The voice commenced by revealing herself by title, a title that brought with it an invitation of mystery and intrigue.

"The Bee Mistress knows *the Power of the Six, the command of the hexagon, the vessel of the bee—our* hexagramma mysticum—*the sweet six-sided honeycomb, one of the great geniuses of the hive, a signature of the honeybee's acute intelligence. This shape and configuration held within each individual cell we know as the shape most efficient within our cosmos. Consider the geometrical exactitude required and imagine—if you can, Initiate— any other format or pattern of cell where no empty space would exist between them. You cannot, for no such shape exists. Within our hexagramma mysticum, all space is utilized in full; no gap may arise. What might this say to you about our community and the way that we are in relationship with one another?*

With the hexagramma mysticum, the number six is both king and queen; it is the number of exquisite and perfect equilibrium. You are close now to your connection to a miracle of nature—the golden proportion, which manifests the optimal relationships among all the constituent parts of a whole, of the hive. This renders possible and favors the harmonious growth and development of all living things."

In the temporary lull that followed, I had an urge to feel around the hexagon I was in. It seemed such a natural place to find myself, but under the most preternatural and incongruous of circumstances. I was held within a wicker hexagonal construction some four feet in height and three feet in diameter, a distinctive shape that encouraged either a curled, fetuslike position or a squatted, haunched stance, with head slightly bowed. I had learned to feel comfortable within it, the way a fakir learns to feel comfortable on a bed of nails, a marked unease giving way to unexpected gratitude. Beneath me, upon the base of the structure, was a thick layer of dull yellow beeswax that had gradually lost its firmness, becoming progressively more pliable as it absorbed my body heat. This brought about a kneading and molding of the wax against my shape. It now held my form, supporting my body and surrounding it in a rich, waxy aroma.*

---

* The resistance of beeswax to heat is astonishing: It will endure a temperature of 140 degrees Fahrenheit before it melts.

As I inched around the cell of transcendental geometry, following the floating word-shapes that told me of the influence of
the cells' physical shape upon an organism, I continued to
explore the structure with my empirical fingertips, as if I were
reading an ancient codex, a sort of bee braille. Is what I touch
exterior? Am I inside it or it inside me?

The voice of shapes and sighs returned.

"The Bee Mistress knows *that this six-sided pattern is of enormous significance beyond its physical efficiency. Across the world,
six-sided quartz crystals that terminate at a single point have been used
throughout time. Why? Because they are a mirror of the bee cell. The
forces with which Earth creates these hexagonal crystals is contained
within every human being, the human body being full of quartz, in
fluid form. Indeed, our life as human beings is dependent on the fact
that the body continuously wants to form six-sided crystals. Our
planet creates six-sided quartz crystals and the bee makes six-sided
cells; and our needs for this form, and the force that it contains, are the
same. The bee is the creature that can best create this six-sided effect on
other things, because the bee collects from nature the very form of nourishment that can carry over into our bodies this same hexagonally acting form, a force that produces a six-sided effect. The significance of
being placed within such a six-sided structure—such as the one in
which you are now housed—is that it has certain qualities, certain
powers that have a very specific effect on its tenant, as its tenant inter-
nalizes and informs the six-sided form. The reason you have been
placed within this structure is so that your relationship with the bee*

*will be stronger; in the future, the bee will see that you have the same
amount of six-sided power as it has."*

I was alone again. My fingers traced the warp and weft of the
six-sided sanctuary; skill and care had gone into its construction,
an example of the marriage of art and architecture. I reflected on
the words spoken, how spiritual elevation or degradation can
depend on form, and how form can be controlled to achieve harmony. I wondered whether I was this hexagon's first resident,
and if not, what fate befell my predecessor. Would I, like the
Englishman in the story "The Man with the Green Weeds," be
found dead, having dared to test the truth of the saying that anyone who spent a night in a particular magical chair would be by
morning either mad, dead, or a poet?

Time passed and again the voice of shapes returned to her
discourse.

"The Bee Mistress knows *the secret glyph of this tradition is the
lemniscate, the lemniscus infinitorum. Shaped like a figure eight on its
side, or a knot, or the bow of a ribbon, it is commonly known as the
infinity symbol. But it is no mere symbol, Initiate. It has practical
expression as the signature and living pathway of infinity itself,
brought into existence by a billion billion bees. It is the Dance of the
Bee, and we dance this dance with them, as if grabbing the tail of a
comet that takes us outside the circles of time where everything that
ever will happen and everything that ever has happened is happening, simultaneously. We of the Path of Pollen are concerned with
infinity and admire the powers of abstraction that enabled our pred-*

ecessors to think the virtually unthinkable, which is what occurs when one takes on infinity. But we are not bothered with the same questions as the philosophers, the problems and controversies about the ∞ and whether infinite quantities can actually exist as math-ematical entities. The symbol gives us the means of being without ending and the path into and out of that being-without-ending. Remember Hamlet counting himself 'king of infinite space'? This refers to nothing more complicated than mere size—physical space—which is of small consideration for those who can move from this world to the next and the next and the next. We deal with dif-ferent dimensions of infinity, a multiplicity of infinities, which for us carry an endless fascination—and the lemniscate is our cognitive map of the realms revealed.

"To commence your work with the lemniscate, consider that it is composed of a clockwise circle and a counterclockwise circle, a solar right side and a lunar left side. In other words, it consists of both right-hand and left-hand paths. This will tell you something of the nature of the Path of Pollen: We traverse both paths. It is also the symbol of the twin—the dark one and the bright one, and the fertile communion that can exist between them. It denotes sexual union between male and female, the two becoming one. It also indicates the path that internal energy may be induced to follow within the body to induce the flight of the bee, the dance of the serpent, and, within women, the flowing of nectars woven with another person or object—a star or a planet, for instance. It is the circuit of force. It is also the symbol of the joining of two cultures—human and bee—and the symbiotic relationship that can exist between them. Note that *neither circle lies above the other, and thus equality in relationship is implied, leading to intimate knowledge of the infinite. It is the pathway we use to receive wisdom from the hive and it is how we implant our knowings into the hive, the asking and the telling of the bees, indicating the influx and emanation of wisdom, both into the hive and emanating from it, in a constant flow of wisdom. It is the World Tree upon which we ascend and descend and sail to the other worlds. It is a dance that those on the Path of Pollen dance, when men and women gather to work together."*

As she spoke of the dance, I recalled that even as a young child I would absentmindedly walk the infinity walk on pavements and playgrounds. Now the Bee Mistress was telling me that it represented a means to explore hidden realms.

"It is also how life arrived here; it is the arrival of the multiplicity of life onto our Earth, and within it is held the six-rayed star, the caduceus within the hands of Mercury, the golden chain of Homer, the serpent coiled on the cross of Tao, the Ouroboros with no beginning or end, the vesica piscis, the Tree of Life, the harmonic proportions of woman and man and the serpent energies that may rise and fall within them."

There was a sudden hush, followed by what sounded like her tracing the symbol on each of the six sides of the hexagon. The sensation that accompanied this was that these were ∞ simultaneously being tattooed or burned onto my skin and then moving through my body like an underground fire, all six lemniscates conjoining within my spine, spinning, rising, and

74

falling like snakes in coitus. A fire and ecstasy rose up to become an atrocious voltage, and I was as ripe wax from the combs. I liquefied under the burning gaze of the ∞. And in this smelting, I fused with, embodied, in-bodied, the ⬡ .

I awoke with narrow lines of sunlight streaming through the spaces in my home, dissolving the darkness. The sun had kept its promise and had risen again. And as the hibernating bear knows when the time has arrived to leave its mossy hollow upon the dawn of spring, so I knew that it was my time to leave. I paused for a moment to feel the comfort of my animal warmth and prepare myself to emerge from my sanctuary. Pushing aside the blanket that had served as the roof of my home, I rose up and stretched out like a cat. I looked upon the genial structure as I stood within its center, fascinated by its construction and its role. I felt utterly different, not just in mind but in body also. Presumably due to my pollen diet, I had lost some fifteen pounds of puppy fat that had tenaciously clung to me since childhood. But I also felt more vital, more animated and alive than I could ever recall.

Climbing out of the structure, I glanced at a mirror hanging above the small fireplace. Was that my face? It was almost unknown to me, emanating a vital brightness that belonged to a solar realm I did not know as my own.

A shining, cloudless, crisp January morning was hinting

through the partially drawn curtains, and I exited the room and made my way to the back of the house and out the back door with its pointed arch. Bridge was sitting on the porch. As I came out of the house, a bird came soaring from beneath the arches supporting the roof; it, too, had found its gateway to the light.

The wind was warm and welcoming. This was a new world.

"Twenty-three days." Bridge spoke gently as he rose to hug me. He held me tight as my body instinctively pulled back in astonishment that I had been enclosed for nearly a month. "Twenty-three days and nights you have been cooked, and quite a feast you would appear to be—and a lean one at that! Twenty-three days and nights," he repeated, "exactly the time it takes for the drone to emerge fully formed from the cell."

As he continued his embrace, he whispered the words "I dreamt I was a bee and when I awoke I wondered if perhaps I was a bee dreaming I was a man." Bridge knew of my love of Kafka, and, indeed, in some fashion my initiation echoed the tragicomic myth of Kafka's *Metamorphosis*, in which Gregor Samsa awakens one morning to find he has been transformed into a giant dung beetle. To me this story summed up the sometimes terrifying absurdity of reality as well as the pitfalls of seeking self-transformation. But I could not dismiss my experience as easily as that, and Bridge's words shook me, for with them he was informing me that the experience I endured had been anticipated, even expected—that he knew of the intricacies and challenges of my journey. Rather, it was as if my own metamorphosis into a bee was already foreknowledge, for I had not told him of

it, and yet here he was referring to the "dream" of being a bee—
or, I wondered, now that I was "awakened," was it, instead a
dream of manhood on the part of a dreaming bee?

"Contact with what is timeless does not leave you as you
were. It cannot; you have had your past taken from you, Twig.
Your old life is gone, and you have been reborn with a new destiny, a second destiny—born again, adopted by the hive.

"You have now envisioned for yourself something of the
magic of this path. Magic has a poor reputation, primarily
because the sublime science of our ancestors has too often
served the wrong master. But it would seem that you are in the
right place, my son." He dropped his embrace and stood opposite me, smiling warmly and nodding.

"You are now upon the Path of Pollen. You have dared to
take initiatives contrary to the laws of life, embraced them, and
survived—in fine fettle, no less! In doing so, you have unleashed
the tempest, which will be calmed only by what emanates from
your heart—the expression of authentic wisdom. Twig, every
man and woman has his or her own vocation. The talent is in
hearing the call, and you have heard the call."

5

The Web of Dreams

I have spread my dreams under your feet;
Tread softly because you tread on my dreams.

W. B. Yeats,
"Aedh Wishes for the Clothes of Heaven"

We sat on the porch and slipped into busy silence, during which much was said regarding our relationship; it was solidified and our trajectory together confirmed.

Bridge broke the silence by suggesting that I bathe to wash away the sweat and grime and tears of my passage, knowing that my next task—self-appointed—would be to visit the orchard, the apiary, the hives, and the bees.

After my bath, I headed out to the orchard. With the Gate of Transition before me once more, and the trepidation of crossing its threshold now long extinct, I passed through, feeling that the mystic green landscape beyond had a far richer connection to my soul. Kipling reverberated through my mind: "Our England is a garden." Here were still, rural regions, peaceful and beloved, where tranquil rivers flowed, rolling meadows shone in the sun, and castles and cathedrals sat serenely, much as they do in the Britain of storybooks. A little farther afield were grim moors, abrupt hills, and threatening islands. And beyond and behind this outer landscape—I now knew this with certainty— there was a hidden world all around me, a world full of magic, mystery, and adventure, and I considered how the character of the British people was molded and informed as much by the quiet secluded valleys and the steep crags as the mysteries that emanate from behind the trembling veil that separates the unseen world from this one.

I quietly entered into the orchard and moved toward, around, and between the hives. Much had changed. In fact, in retrospect it seemed it was this moment when the bees flew into my life most fully, for they alighted upon me, seemingly in wel- come, and danced around me, seemingly with joy, and yes—I could faintly hear the wisdom-hum of the hive. I had heard this gentle buzzing within the cell; it was a familiar resonant tone that heralded the touching of one world to another—the everyday world and a world with a different, non-Aristotelian logic. I was panning the living clay within which I was to unearth gold.

As I listened to the wisdom of the hive, I was barely aware that I was following the route of a single honeybee as she moved from her home out across the air. She descended slowly onto a blue delphinium, braked on a petal, and walked into the flower, which bent slightly as she fell and clung to the blue, turned-down edge. It was heavenly within: an intoxicating perfume amid golden pollen dust that fell around her. She rolled in it, bathed in it, and imbibed the sticky-sweet nectar. After taking her fill, she turned her eyes toward the sun, taking her bearing from it, and started for home. She was so weighted down she could hardly fly, every part of her a mass of golden dust. She hovered over a flower bed, combing and cleaning herself, and crammed the combings into two baskets on her hind legs. Gradually she became clean and, being clean, she longed and lusted for another bath in warm, scented dust.

Another flower bowed to receive her. She visited flower after flower until she could imbibe no more. So laden was she with treasure that her flight home was arduous, but she slowly climbed in altitude and made for the hive, which at last came into view. As she landed, other bees emerged and crowded around her, and an admiring circle escorted her to the combs. She began to dance; it was the infinity dance of the lemniscate, a vigorous, flowing figure eight, a magical pattern I was to emulate time and again across the coming months, a dance that would eventually take me outside the circles of time.

I spent the next handful of days with Bridge as he watched over me. It was a classical debriefing undertaken by the Bee Master, a planned interaction that included critical examination, review, and discussion on the outcome of events. It contained a sharing of previously undisclosed information to ensure that any misconceptions were clarified and settled.

Bridge knew how to gut a report very quickly—how to get to

the inner, essential part of anything—and I was given further instruction and, in turn, elucidation of my experiences, reviewing what I understood about the *hexagramma mysticum* and the *lemniscus infinitorum*. Bridge made it clear that both of these glyphs not only have their own diagram, but they also possess their own meditation, sound, form, and actions.

"This tradition carries evocative symbolism, Twig, that always finds a practical expression, for from its *use* a language is made. This symbolism has descended through diverse streams from immense antiquity within this initiatory path, proceeding both from the immediate vision of the individual initiate and from the historical succession and wisdom of the tradition."

Bridge requested that I describe the entire episode in precise detail. I groped for words as I attempted to relate what I considered to be a barely communicable, highly subjective experience. In turn, I was able to ask whatever questions I wanted, without a single mention of low-hanging fruit!

Bridge explained what had happened: With the aid of the bees and the venom, he had moved my awareness—my total being—into the world of the bee. He explained that the process involved using bee venom on certain points on the human body, which a bee practitioner can manipulate through the application of the sting. These key points form a unified field. If one traced a line between these points, an internal area where the body's energy moves continually would remain. The venom was administered on the perimeter of this space, and in addition Bridge used his ability to push people into transcendental realms. The final point where Bridge stung me—the area known by shamans as the Strong Eye, the point between the eyebrows—is of particular importance in bee medicine, a place known simply as Reveals. It is considered crucial because the blood of the head runs through it, and it also opens the way for initiates, aligning as it does with the mysterious eyes of the bee.

Beyond the loss of body weight, there were two other changes in my appearance that were seemingly related to my induction into the bee cultus. First, I had developed what turned out to be a permanent line running down my forehead, like a frown line but running on the diagonal. "The first of your two antennae, antennae of the soul." Bridge laughed as he pointed to two barely visible lines running down his own forehead, which met and intersected below the area of the Strong Eye. The other peculiarity that became apparent over the next few months was that my hair, which had curled and waved since boyhood, began to grow straight. "Tresses of the bee, young Twig, tresses of the bee!" Bridge would comment. I attempted to dismiss his remark, for the idea that I had not only begun to see the world quite differently, but that my body also had undergone changes, unnerved and disturbed me more than I was prepared to admit.

When I finished describing my induction experience, Bridge suggested that my sleeping patterns might fluctuate. This occurrence, he said, was an optimum time to relinquish the familiarity of a bed and step into the *dreaming web*, which I knew as the hammock. According to Bridge, the hammock originated thousands of years ago. It was used by members of the Path of Pollen not only for rest, but also for *oneiric* work. I learned that oneiricism—which relates to dreams and dreaming—played a vital role in the Path of Pollen, and that the hammock was considered to be the ideal vessel for this work. This explained why there was only a single bed within the house, in the guest bedroom.

Bridge informed me that the structure in which I had been placed during my initiation was also used for dreaming work, usually following initiatory rites of passage. He called the structure a oneiricell (from the Greek *oneiros*, "dream"), the cell of dreaming, a large-scale replica of the individual cell of the honeybee. He added, with laughter in his eyes, that the weavers of baskets were originally known as Twiggies, and he suggested that it was only a matter of time before I went from being a mere Twig to becoming a member of the Guild of Twiggies. However, it was the dreaming web I used on a daily basis, and Bridge's instruction on how to use it showed me yet again what a practical technician of the sacred he was.

Bridge explained that the dreaming web evolved from the dream work developed by certain Greek mystery schools that perfected the art of incubation dream-sleep. The individual would be placed within a specially built chamber that was housed in a temple usually dedicated to Asklepios, the Greek god of healing, and within this incubation chamber he or she

84

would receive by way of dreaming the appropriate visitation from the gods and subsequent healing.*

"We use a particular method of dreaming when we sleep, so that our time on Earth—a brief moment in the middle of eternity—is not wasted," Bridge continued. In passing, Bridge mentioned that in the 1860s, the Methodist minister Reverend Langstroth had a heavenly revelation while dreaming that detailed how to construct the first beehive with self-spacing removable frames, for which he was named the father of modern beekeeping. "European traditions of dreaming are perhaps more hidden than those elsewhere. Dream work reached its peak in the Greek mystery schools, where they developed Asklepian dream incubation, which was active for almost two millennia. Our practice of true dreaming and dream hunting was built on this tradition. It is a potent process of accessing other realities and, when undertaken with acute vigilance, it brings about a controlled awareness of our dream-life." Bridge rolled out a hammock and attached it to two hooks on the wall. "Observe and learn," he instructed, and I stood aside as he deftly climbed onto the hammock, lay down, and gripped its sides.

He began to swing like a pendulum and then shifted his weight sharply, sending the hammock whirling like a spinning

---

* These temples were not restricted to Greece. In later years, Bridge and I visited a dream incubation temple in Britain—the Temple of Nodens near Lydney in Gloucestershire, which Bridge believed had been used as a Keltic place of dream work before the Romans arrived.

wheel, which had the effect of totally enclosing his body within the hammock material. It slowed to a standstill, and Bridge was hidden within this cocoon. From that evening on, I adapted to this mode of entering into sleep.

Bridge also insisted that I now operate left-handed. I was naturally right-handed, but Bridge urged me to disengage from this, as the work of the Path of Pollen, he reminded me, was a marriage of both the Left-Hand Path and the Right-Hand Path. In recognition of this, a high degree of what I understood as ambidexterity was required by those who "sailed the lemniscate." Bridge explained, "The idea of 'handedness' is a unique feature of humans, Twig. It is a physical symptom of the dominance and preference of one side over the other. I want you to be able to operate with both your right hand and your left hand. But I would not call this ambidextrous, which simply means two right hands, which to me would be no better than having two left feet!" I silently disposed of the word in the now rapidly filling wastebasket of old meanings.

"Did you know, Twig, that the Catholic Church at one point declared that being left-handed made you a servant of the devil?" Bridge asked me. "In many languages, the word *left* is associated with trouble and the diabolical. In fact, the term *sinister* translates from the Latin as left. But in truth, left-handers excel in certain tasks and professions, notably higher math, chess, music, draftsmanship, and art. Leonardo da Vinci, Michelangelo, Raphael, and Picasso were all left-handed. So let us see what occurs if we enforce the left side upon you."

The terms Right-Hand Path and Left-Hand Path were, he elaborated, specific and technical terms derived from Indo-European tantric practices. The Right-Hand Path is distinguished from the Left in that it does not include a sexual component, whereas the Left-Hand Path allows sexual intercourse as part of its work. "It is a passage by way of the senses; the eyes, the heart, and the spontaneity of the body—it is these that assist us in arriving at the point of central stillness upon our turning world. It has been remarked that the negative connotations of being left-handed are largely due to a battle of the sexes, for most if not all myths agree that the right side is male and the left side female. No doubt you are aware that the left hemisphere of the brain, which controls the right side of the body, is said to evolve logical thought sequences and suppress sensory input that might interfere with problem solving. The right hemisphere, governing the left side of the body, is often called the intuitive, creative, or imaginative part of the brain. It is supposed to generate the more sensitive awareness made manifest in feelings, empathy, art, visual imagery, and inspiration, qualities that certain people consider aspects of the female."

This was obviously an oversimplification, but Bridge wanted me to be drawing on those aspects so that I could step into "all of who you are," and he instructed me in a technique of balancing both hemispheres of the brain. The method involved me holding out my right arm directly in front of me, with my forefinger "pointing toward infinity." I then began to draw the lemniscate figure in the air, approximately four feet across in size, ever keeping my eye on the precise spot where my finger was, and at the same time seeing the lemniscate forming in my mind's eye. I then repeated this with the other arm. Whatever it may have done in balancing the two sides of my brain, it would always offer me an extended and heightened level of awareness. This basic shape making went on to more elaborate forms of working with the ∞ as a means of exercising the physical form, so that each limb and muscle group was exercised, always working in the pattern of the lemniscate, and including a dance that was an emulation of the dance that the bee undertakes. In time, this gave way to embracing the finer art of orbiting the lemniscate around the interior of the body, within vital organs and bone groups, linking the interior stars to one another and to the spine, so that a caduceus was formed, the spinal column becoming the central column of the caduceus.

The process of becoming bidextrous was initiated with having my right arm tied to my back. Just as an eye patch might be worn over one eye to force the use of the weaker, "lazy" eye, which then becomes stronger with use, so the function of my right arm was removed from me, leaving me with no choice but to use my left hand. This harsh procedure was accompanied by actively putting my attention on my left side and completely ignoring the right-hand side of my body as much as possible. Over a period of seven days, I was to localize my sense of self, the "I," in a different limb on the left side, changing the point of my focus every twenty-four hours. After a week of this, my imprisoned arm was released. Within the space of those few days, the left arm had become the dominant side. My entire musculoskeletal organization had changed.

Bridge then had me mirror writing, again with the left hand. Mirror writing is writing from right to left and reversed so that the result appears normal when reflected in a mirror. Leonardo wrote most of his manuscripts, letters, and meticulously illustrated note-books in mirror image. (No one knows why he wrote this way; two theories have suggested convenience and security.)

After some eight months of not using my right hand for writing, working with the hives, or any other daily physical activity, I seemed to reach a crossover point where my mind became unsure which hand to use. After that, a more balanced ability emerged, and from that moment on I was able to move my hands with remarkable synchronicity.

During this time I also integrated much that had occurred during my initiation, and I was now seldom troubled by what I had been through. I had arrived at a simple knowing that I had direct contact with an indefinitely ancient yet ever new hive gnosis, and that I belonged within the hive as one of its sons, as well as outside the hive as an ambassador of the queen. I also, during this period, received instruction on the theory and appli-cation of bee venom and the interior stars, and I deepened into my dreaming practice within the web.

Another part of my training was the study of time, which Bridge introduced to me in his typically riddlish fashion, just after I had worked particularly well with the hives (or so I thought): "Twig, you know that anyone is capable of getting a few things right. Even a stopped clock is right twice a day! But what does the clock tell us? What, in fact, is time?" I pointed to my watch, but before I could open my mouth, Bridge retorted, "Does time wear a watch? Twig, one phenomenon you've witnessed is that of time dilation. Reflect for a moment on your *time* within the hive; you were born, lived, and died the life of a drone, but in the ordinary world of time, you had left this world for just a few short hours. Conversely, when you emerged from your time within the oneiricell, you were aghast to learn that you had been within it for over three weeks."

I was reminded of the basic theory of time dilation as held by the scientific community—that if, for example, a craft were to approach the speed of light, time would slow down for anyone traveling within it. A variety of experiments have proved this, the most common of which involves using a pair of clocks. One of the two clocks is placed in a jet plane that sets off at high speed. The other clock remains static on the ground. When the airplane returns and the two clocks meet, the clock that was on the plane is now running a short amount of time *behind* the one that remained stationed on the earth. The theory of special relativity proved that a moving clock will tick more slowly than when it is at rest, and that by attaining the speed of light, time will come to a complete standstill.

Bridge continued: "Throughout history, human beings have been fighting a losing battle against time, and tales abound of folk seeking to prolong their lives using a variety of means. These people have been looking in the wrong direction. The function of clocks is to chop up the twenty-four hours of the day more or less reliably into hours, minutes, and seconds. This might be called objective time, because all the watches in the world are supposed to cut time into slices of even thickness. However, we know that time does not feel as if it is passing evenly under different circumstances: Time may fly or time may drag. When Einstein was asked about this phenomenon, he replied that if he spent two hours with a beautiful woman, it flew by in a minute, but if he sat on a hot cooker for just a minute, it felt like two hours! Einstein was a true scientist, not afraid of giving mention to the gods. But you know, Twig, the science exploring the mysteries of time was already undertaken by our ancestors and by those who blazed the trail before us. Vigilance and determination alone are required."

The Bee Master got up to collect his tanging quoit, and I wondered if he was about to reveal the secret of immortality to me, or at least that of longevity. He played upon the quoit for some minutes and all the while I was made to stare at the second hand of a clock. And so I waited, watching the clock. At a certain moment, when I was slipping into the state I used to commune with the hive, the second hand came to a stop! My immediate response to this was that it was impossible, and at that moment the second hand began to accelerate once again and resume its normal rate. With further training—primarily not reacting to what my eyes were witnessing—using vigilance and determination, I could get to the point where I could keep the second hand from moving for as long as I wished.

I learned that time is not like the proverbial arrow, moving ever forward at a constant and steady velocity, but is rather more like the waters upon the earth. Within great oceans of ever-changing time, multiple forms of life ebb and flow through waves, surface currents, and what Bridge called "deep time circulation." Elsewhere small fathomless pools of time move imperceptibly. Time may rage and rain and storm. It may be still and, yes, it can stagnate. Time can be absorbed through the cracks in the rocks of matter—and in dry and arid deserts of the cosmos it may be absent altogether. The rivers of time move one way, only to then move another.

The next stage of this work was undertaken alone and involved my beginning to physically move about once the second hand had stopped ticking—a process that took several years to master on the most elementary level. It took enormous levels of concentration to initiate this work and get to the point when a first step could be taken without the world starting to move again, but over a period of months I began to do this in a limited fashion.

Having reached a basic working level, Bridge informed me that the next stage was for him to be present. At the appointed hour, when dusk held out its arms to the darkness, I stepped into what Bridge called "the halting" and began to move around the room where everything had become suspended in time. It was no great surprise to find that this in no way interfered with

Bridge, who moved into this place seamlessly and improved my abilities with his presence alone. We ventured out beneath the blue-black sky, and, indeed, the world had stopped: There was no sound but our breathing, no movement but our own. Surely the earth still turned? Within the world that Bridge and I inhabited, time was not. Being in no-time with Bridge became some of my most treasured memories of him, yet I reached levels of proficiency only after nearly a decade of our work together.

Exactly one year had gone by since my initiation. Once again we were together on the last day of the old year, sitting around his wood-burning stove, having shared a meal of Welsh mountain lamb that Bridge served with homemade mustard flavored with mead, rose hips, and herbs. He cooked as if it was the last thing he would do—as indeed he did everything—and thus he gave himself to it utterly and without reservation.

"Twig." Bridge uttered my name quietly. "Twig, you are now my kith and kin. As you continue to deepen into the Path of Pollen, your task is to become detached but not indifferent— serene but not inactive. With that in mind, you should continue to make progress upon this path, even as an Englishman."

"That's a very sweeping statement, Bridge!" I exclaimed at his remark regarding my nationality. At that, he moved across the room and passed me a broom, murmuring in a droll tone, "But Twig, sweeping can be a most worthwhile activity."

6

The Bee Mistress and the Melissae

Loving is a journey with water and with stars,
with smothered air and abrupt storms of flour:
loving is a clash of lightning-bolts
and two bodies defeated by a single drop of honey.

PABLO NERUDA, "SONNET XII,"
ONE HUNDRED LOVE SONNETS

I felt her presence, a sort of gossamer lightness at the back of me, before I ever saw or heard her. I had been watching intently as several bees worked their way along the flower of a southern marsh orchid. This was one of Bridge's many instructions, designed to hone the practice of observing not just with the eyes, but with the entire body as well, of entering the world of the bee so that one could come to understand its rituals and energy. I was so focused on this task that I had not noticed that one of the mysterious women I had heard about but never encountered—the Melissae—had entered the apiary and quietly made her way over to stand behind me. She had watched in silence as I continued my observations and then, lightly, she whispered (clearly to me, but as if into the flower itself): "Is the flower the food of the bee—or is the bee the genitals of the flower?"

The voice encompassed all manner of depth and emotion, an intoxicating melting of sound within which clarity and strength could be heard, yet there was also a rich and deep sensuality, an earthiness. There was laughter in her voice, too— whether at me or at her comment I wasn't sure—that further served to displace me in her presence, consumed by her as I had become in a stretch of time that would barely register on a clock. And there was more still in these layers of sound that unraveled before me, an accent I could not quite place but that spoke of the mysteries beyond the Carpathian Mountains, tinged with luminosity from vast Arizona skies.

This was my introduction to the Melissae, six female apprentices of a formidable woman known to me only by her formal title, the Bee Mistress.

This Melissa was veiled, in the way of all the Melissae. The overt reason for the black netting was to protect the women from the bees, but there was a deeper purpose, too: to protect them from prying eyes and to safeguard their mystery.

Perhaps not surprisingly, I was utterly enchanted by these mysterious women who were never seen without their veils, and it seemed I had been either inadvertently or deliberately kept away from them, for at every opportunity that I felt I would finally be introduced to them, they withdrew as if on silent command. Bridge refused to elaborate on the matter; he would merely mutter, in barely audible tones, that "the wind cannot be caught in a net," and he would speak of "pouring water into a sieve"—words that beguiled me further and strengthened the magnetic pull these women seemed to have. It took many hours over many months to discover even the most basic information about them. I now know that my questions and increasingly frantic probes were utterly unsuccessful in any case, for the few crumbs of information that were given to me were, in retrospect, quite deliberately metered out in near-homeopathic dosages. Of course, this had merely served to excite me more—an excitement matched only by my exasperation.

Bridge finally gave in to my need for information when I asked him in a frustrated tone, "Well, what on earth is their purpose—if they actually have one, that is." Seemingly without moving a muscle, he swung around, met my eyes, and began to speak. *"The Bee Master knows* that the knowledge of destiny and the ability to inspire are two of the central powers of these women. The knowledge of destiny, however, is much more than simple folk-magic; it is the innate knowledge of *type,* and it includes the ability to educate and guide a type according to the sort of power that type is meant to have."

I was left hanging as to what a "type" was. I assumed it was a form of personality or human nature, and that the Melissae could somehow attune themselves to this in order to offer guidance and instruction that was most suited to that particular person. This assumption only served to exasperate me more, of course, and to raise other niggling questions: What type, then, was I? And what form might my own education with these women take, should I ever be lucky enough to actually meet them?

To my surprise and delight, on this occasion Bridge continued to elaborate: "The Melissae are women who live in a country that is east of the sun and west of the moon and for which there is no known map. Like the bee herself, they are veil-winged creatures, human hymenopteran." I could not help but note the reference to the hymen, or veil, that, in addition to its more common application, referred to the covering of the inner shrine of the Goddess's temple, and I wondered what, if any, relevance this might have to the Melissae's purpose.

"We—men—are 'guests' of the bee tradition, and the Melissae are our hosts, for bee society represents the zenith of the feminine potency of nature. We are mere drones, Twig, and you'd best be remembering that. *Rex non utitur aculeo!** The basics of masculinity and femininity have not changed much in a million years; the female consistently does more of the reproductive work and the male is, in many ways, a parasite upon his partner. Women may be the last thing to be 'civilized' by men, and these women—these wild ones—will never be, and those who have fallen into their arms rarely do so without falling into their hands.

---

* This Latin phrase translates as "The king has no sting." It was used by Louis XII of France in 1506, appearing on his breastplate, which was further edged with golden bees and beehives.

"They carry arcane skills that allow them to pacify, subjugate, paralyze, obstruct, and even dream a man's death, should they so wish. But Twig, if you were to meet these women, I wonder if you would even notice them, for 'civilized' man stamps and frets along his little rut into his grave, never looking around at the beauty, savagery, emotion, and wonder that he rushes blindly past. The eye sees only what the mind is prepared to comprehend, and so, Twig, my question is, would you even see them, were they to be in your presence? Or perhaps I should say that you have yet to perceive them when they have chosen to be around you, for they tread softly and whisper in the ear, they glide to and fro and in and out, concealed beneath whatever mask best serves their ends."

Despite the enigma of his words regarding the role of men in the tradition, I sensed they were meant to prepare me and may not be presenting the most complete picture. It seemed to me that the role of the Bee Master and Bee Mistress and the connection between them was not based on who was the superior of the two, but that both roles were distinct and of equal importance, their functions together performing a corporate responsibility. Beyond that, I allowed my fantasies to shape these women as members of an ancient tradition of committed people able to work in ways that were outside the known laws of science, so that their activities were transformed into cosmic events that could influence the world around them and nourish the inner life of each generation.

Bridge continued his talk on the distaff members of the

tradition as we moved around the apiary. *"The Bee Master knows that there are seven who serve, a hexad of apprentices and their teacher, known respectively as the Melissae and the Bee Mistress, who is known by her charges as the Mother Bee and by the Bee Masters as the Queen of Synchronicity. Perhaps one day you will discover why we bestowed this title upon her. You are aware that the Bee Master instructs one male apprentice at a time, but the Bee Mistress instructs six female apprentices—six being the primary number of power in this sacred tradition, based in part on the hexagonal shape of the cells within the hive. The Bee Mistress is referred to as the Mother Bee after the goddess Demeter, who governed the cycles of all life during the time when she was a most revered goddess and when the cultus of the bee was public. The gods and goddesses are like politicians, Twig: Their power and influence depend on the size and strength of their constituency. Eventually, as their constituency diminishes, they begin to fade, but the ancient ones associated with our way are kept alive by the Melissae's devotion."*

Bridge then began to tell of the concealed history of the Melissae. He said that they were physical representatives of a hidden sisterhood known as the Sisterhood of the Hive, which was seemingly even more ancient than the Melissae and was extant across the living Earth. "These Melissae are transmitters of an archaic impulse that is central to the Path of Pollen and that reached a mood of excellence during the historical period of the Melissae of Grecian temple traditions, holding links with the great oracular center of Delphi, which was a center of focus for the ancient feminine powers ruled over by the dragoness Delphine. The term Melissae has continued to be used by those women who work within the tradition in Europe, and the Sisterhood of the Hive is the collective name for all women who work in this way, regardless of where upon the planet."

The word Melissa translates simply as bee. The first Melissa was said to have cared for the infant Zeus while he was being hidden from his father, the king of all the Gods. Melissa plundered beehives in order to feed honey to Zeus. When Melissa's role in protecting Zeus was discovered, she was turned into what was considered a lowly species of insect, and Zeus later took pity on her and turned her into a honeybee, forever involved with making honey. "However," Bridge continued, "there is rather more to the work than taking care of gods and making honey, or let us say there is rather more to this tale if seen through *our* eyes. Melissa was also the goddess of intoxication and sexual passion, both of which may be used as doorways to a communion with all of life, and this is the archaic impulse they continue to transmit. Consider, Twig, that the bee is the *copula* between the male and female elements in a flower. We also know the bee can be a beacon for souls, guiding the dead on their way to the next worlds— a psychopomp." Suddenly Bridge came to a halt. "Enough for today," he stated firmly, closing the door on any further discussion. The Knowledge Lecture was complete, but it had served to increase my sense of mystery and intrigue, and it left me wanting at least a few more clues as to the identity of these women and their connection to Bridge and, by implication, to me.

That night I dreamt that I met with the Bee Mistress, who partially removed her clothing and revealed her breasts, which she indicated I should suckle upon. Milk came from one breast and honey flowed from the other. The next morning I told Bridge of my dream, and he reminded me that Britain was once known as the isle of honey—Yr Fel Ynys—or the land of milk and honey, which indicated that the land was healthy, for the people of old knew that both milk and honey are strongly connected with a healthy human life force.

Early the next morning, I wandered into the garden and found an austere presence dressed in black, awaiting my arrival before the Gate of Transition. She was as the Thirteenth Wise Woman who stands as guardian of the threshold, the paradoxical adversary without whose presence no threshold may be passed. And she required no introduction. It was the Queen of Synchronicity who waited, despite my unannounced arrival.

I caught my breath, as if breathing too hard might dispel the vision. But she was quite real. She looked at me with a silent and careful scrutiny, which had the immediate effect of sharpening my own concentration. Silence and sunlight were blankets around us, warm and soporific, and yet simultaneously a penetrating tension sliced the air, an unease at odds with the solar splashes that pooled like liquid gold around her feet. High overhead, in the purple elm blossom, I was faintly aware of the bees and the autumn wind orchestrating nature's music. Higher still, a ripple of lark song hung in the blue, and a score of rooks were sailing by, filling the morning with their rich, deep clamor of unrest.

The Bee Mistress had drawn off her veil in thoughtful deliberation, and with a single finger beckoned me to her. She was of
indeterminate age, anywhere between forty and seventy. I had
observed this phenomenon before, that certain women who
work with spiritual power and outside of time take on a near
timeless quality. She stood at about five and a half feet, with the
chiseled face of an athlete, an olive complexion, and eyes that
had the glint of opals, giving her gaze an intensity that was
simultaneously alluring and alarming. Her long, blue-black hair
clung to her like seaweed and came to rest at the small of her
back. Her voice was inflected by a depth of baritone I have not
before or since heard in a woman's voice. The tempo was equally
extraordinary. Each sentence began with words that moved like
a cat, slowly and precisely circumventing objects to be stalked
and slain or leapt away from at a second's notice, and then with
the same feline knowing she would accelerate to a staccato
rhythm, colored and punctuated with the nuances of an Eastern
European accent within which lay precise grammatical English,
indicating a certain education. I now witnessed the being that
held the voice of shapes and sighs.

"Bridge has sent you, so I suppose I had better take a look at
you," she said with a certain disdain, as if I were an interruption
to her work and a necessary waste of her time, which I suddenly
feared I probably was. And in what sense had I been sent? If
Bridge had a reputation for being matter-of-fact, perhaps even
blunt, the Bee Mistress was his perfect foil.

"I want you to show me what you have learned from the Bee

Master," she continued, referring to her opposite by formal title, all the while eyeing me somewhat doubtfully. "But first, I suppose it is time you met my Melissae." My heart leapt in anticipation, although I did my best to hold a poker face and offered her a simple nod, to which she raised one inquisitive eyebrow and chuckled low in her throat.

We moved into the orchard and I closed the gate behind me. This done, I turned to follow the Bee Mistress, and what I witnessed began, I felt, to spin me into a myth. Here and there in the shade-dappled orchard, figures were moving, at work among the hives, figures of women clad in long gowns with either purple or crimson borders. All of them wore the protective black bee veils, thus I could hazard only the dimmest guess at the faces beneath them, although I thought I recognized the Melissa who had surprised me that day and then disappeared as swiftly as she had appeared. An occasional ripple of laughter broke the busy silence and the Melissa nearest to me—young and of a delicate prettiness, I could have sworn, although her veil disclosed provokingly little—was singing the sweetest of seductive Siren chants as she stooped over an open hive and lifted out a crowded honeycomb. I hoped it was sung for my benefit.

> *The taste of honey is on your lips,*
> *my darling; your tongue is milk and honey for me.*
> *I have entered my garden,*
> *my sweetheart, my bride.*
> *I am gathering my spices and myrrh;*

I am eating my honey and honeycomb;
I am drinking my wine and milk.
Eat, lovers, and drink
until you are drunk with love . . .*

Another of the Melissae was painting a new hive; from what I could see, she was covering it in images of serpents and bees. This was one of the distinguishing features of the Path of Pollen: The hives were hand painted with symbols of power of the Bee Master or Mistress.†

The Bee Mistress noticed me watching this young beekeeper and delivered a sharp look to us both. I was to learn that when the Bee Mistress signaled or called to her charges, no hawks were swifter to her wrist. She molded their characters and left an indelible stamp on their work.

The Melissae all had a curious similarity in build; they were without exception athletic, all sharing a wiry leanness but with no loss of female shape. At the time, I imagined their trimness was due to the sheer physical work involved in their craft, but I

---

* This verse is from the Song of Songs, which is beloved by all the Melissae and chanted regularly when working with the bees.

† The Bee Mistress—being of blood drawn from Latvia, Slovenia, and Lithuania—later told me that certain Slovenian beekeepers also painted their hives—known as *kranjič*—with primal images and religio-magical symbols as well as humorous cartoonlike pictures and stories from their families, a pictorial record of recent family events. I have also been informed that this is done in parts of Africa, and I have witnessed painted hives in Mexico from beekeepers who are not connected to the tradition.

later learned that two of them were sisters who were also genuine athletes, having once worked as circus acrobats and capable of blowing fire and juggling machetes. The others, I would
come to learn, were a lecturer in permaculture (a holistic philosophy of working with nature, based on traditional agricul-
tural practices), a medical doctor turned holistic physician, and
two full-time beekeepers.

Breaking my momentary reverie, the Bee Mistress asked me
to open one of the hives. This was a simple enough operation,
but I had a sense that it was some form of examination; I was on
display and the Melissae were watching me as they went about
their business. It seemed that the rules, the form, the techniques,
and the interactions of these women were all conducted in sign
and body language, with laughter the interpreter.

I approached one of the hives from behind and grasped the
hand grip of the bottom hive body, lifting it to estimate its
weight. It was heavy with honey, which for this time of year was
a good sign. I picked up my smoker and lit it with the reverence
I now knew to be essential; each movement, each motion in this
dance is as important as the next, and nothing is done without
the etiquette of ceremony. I puffed a stream of smoke into the
hive entrance to subdue the guard bees and prevent them from
spreading the alarm, all the while emitting from my lungs a
deep, soulful, rhythmical whistling that conveyed my message
of peace. With my hive tool I loosened the hive's telescoping
cover and removed it, prying up the inner cover and puffing
more smoke into the top of the hive, which was filled with bees

in bustling numbers. They had felt the jarring disturbance, and their abdomens were raised defensively, momentarily ready to sting if necessary. But with the whistling chant taking effect, most began to move down between the frames, with others coming to alight upon my arms. I rested my hand on the frames and felt the warmth of the bees rising upward, the fragile bodies beginning to dance on my hand, several of them depositing the liquid nectar they were carrying onto my palm in communion with the part of me that was they.

Finally, we made the round of the whole busy, murmuring enclosure and came again to the gate. Preparing myself to pass through and out into the consensus world again, the Bee Mistress gave me a final word: "Bridge has not done too bad a job with you, all things considered. I shall be seeing you again." And that was my good-bye.

Just over a month later I was formally summoned to meet with the Bee Mistress, this time in her private rooms within the thick bulging walls of the house and with none of her Melissae present. Bridge had mentioned that I should make every effort to be on time, for the Bee Mistress kept time as punctiliously as an atomic clock and expected others to do so also. Her room was dominated by a huge loom—we were more or less in its shadow—and as with the inscription carved on the Gate of Transition, so a simple word was carved on her door: *audmi*, Lithuanian for weave.

Upon entering, I was aware of the scent of cedar, which I surmised emanated from the loom. I also noticed six chairs set in a hexagonal pattern, facing inward toward an oversized bee skep* that stood about two and a half feet in height and perhaps a little less in diameter. Embroidered cushions lay on every side of the room, and from the rafters hung seven masks, which I began to admire and inspect. ("Worn not to conceal the human, but rather to reveal the god," the Bee Mistress stated quietly.) A huge earthenware oven stood in the far corner, rising from floor to ceiling like a gigantic olive jar, with strings of onions and fat hams hanging in glorious torture from twisted hooks in the ceiling.

She guided me to a conventional and quite comfortable chair, and from a modest blackened cauldron I was offered a glass of *krupnikas*, which she explained was a prized Lithuanian honey liqueur, akin to a mead but with notes of ginger, clove, and nutmeg. Before me I noticed a small collection of cakes on a tray, food to quell my intoxication. They were a curious shape and I could not help but think they were vulval in form, and that perhaps they held some distant link between the Mellisae and those who carried the genital-shaped cakes at the Greek thesmophoria festival that Bridge had described to me, a festi-

---

* A skep is an early type of beehive, usually made of straw in a conical shape. It is often still used as an image on a variety of honey products. Another member of the Path of Pollen, Rainier Hüs, is an expert on how to make skeps, specifically those used in Wales, which are constructed from hazel switches coated in a mixture of lime and cow dung and are more domed than their straw cousins.

val of thanksgiving to honor the goddess Demeter for teaching mankind to tend the soil. The Bee Mistress indicated that they were to be sampled. They smelled of burning peat and tasted of midnight. They were delicious. She then sat herself in a rocking chair and allowed the gentle to and fro to move her as would a boat hewn of English walnut.

Slowly, as if adrift on a rhythmic sea of time and tide, these waves of hers became endless to me, and rocked me into a world of neverness, all the while keeping me anchored in the present. As if I were not intoxicated enough already, I supped from the glass she had handed me—and then the looking glass through which I peered became holographic, complete; I was entirely within it, all my senses consumed. The intricate flavors of the liqueur exposed themselves to me; ginger, clove, and nutmeg washed into me, precise in their target. Every note of this drink had a place to go, though I was lost as to their destination. Only did I know this: I was primed by the drink, ready to receive the heady embrace of the words to come.

I sat in the presence of this Queen Bee, watching as her fingers and her breathing intertwined with the mastery of the mistress who knows the weave of all manner of matter. They aligned themselves to one another—her rocking, her breathing, and the movement of her fingers—until there was nothing, not an atom of air in that room, that was not in harmony. And finally, just at the moment when I thought the air might be taken from my lungs for the simple sake of the concert, she spoke.

"The Bee Mistress knows that everything is born of woman. What is to you the universe is to us the yoni-verse; creation itself is sweet songs of the yoni. The male has never given birth to anything. The male may be a seed, may be the conception, but without the reception and without the creativity, there can be no birth. And so we see the Great Yoni as the Void, as the Eternal Parent holding Great-Grandmother and Great-Grandfather, and we see the very beginning of the teachings that concern alchemical sexuality, where our Earth manifests as the sexual center of our Universe. And so, in the Great Void, there was something within nothing, that pure heart light, energy in mental form, and from that, breath, inhale, inclusion, Great-Grandmother, the female, the egg, the receptive, the creative. And then the exhale, explosion, the seed, the active, the Parent saw itself in its two sides and made love and out of that it created itself in all forms and all things. This is the yoni-verse in which we have our being and that is the context in which I wish you to hear what follows. It is time for you to replace unconfirmed theories, false notions, and abstract opinions with an awareness of the countless links that unite all elements in the rhythm of life. In doing this you may discover our knowing and our vision."

The Queen Bee continued.

"For most people in the West, the yoni is all sin, shame, and fig leaves! This is no passive vessel, but an intelligence, and the work undertaken with this intelligence is our fulcrum. No religion has in practice been good for women; all represent century upon century of oppression. The women within the Path of Pollen are fully empowered. Not empowered in the way that many women are in this day and age, where, in an attempt to gain power that was taken from them, they often become the imitation of men. The sun and Earth do not compete; they are opposites. Look at nature: We see that opposition creates the greater whole, harmony. Competition destroys. The Melissae do not compete with men; rather, they understand that their power as women means they can be sensual, sexual, lusty, passionate, even wanton, and that does not make them an object for you or any other man. In fact, it is their power that gives birth to all things: sexuality, emotion, mind, body, and spirit. Our treasure lies in the beehive of our knowledge, for we are honey-gatherers of the mind.

"The Bee Mistress knows that Melissae fall into two distinct groupings, two primary types drawn to this work: the maternal type and the magnetic type. Each of my daughters, my Melissae, inclines in varying degrees to one or the other of these extremes. If she is purely of the maternal type, she will ask little save to be fecundated year by year, and to protect and provide for her offspring, whether this be a ritual, sacred dream, or indeed a child. If she is of the magnetic type, and if true to the law of her nature, she will deny herself to no one who calls upon her in the name of the tradition. Called by the powers of womanhood within her, she is by nature rootless, solitary, and free moving, and, if true to herself, she does not bind herself even from one hour to another, beyond the perennial communion with the hive. You have met Vivienne, have you not?"

she added, by means of illustration of this type. I was to learn that Vivienne, along with her colleagues Morag and

Katarina, was the magnetic type. Devorah, Fionulla, and Nivetta were of the maternal type. The Bee Mistress then slipped effortlessly into metaphor.

"That is to say, there is one sort of bee who moves from flower to flower, sipping nectar from each luscious blossom. Picking up pollen from this bloom, she deposits it into that one, circulating pollen everywhere, fertilizing all the plants. As a result, the garden flourishes. Back in the hive, she deposits the pollen-rich nectar into communal vats. In the fullness of time this will ripen into honey—dark, rich, and sweet, a visible offering to the visible face of the spirits.

"There is another type of bee who also moves from flower to flower, but does not sip nectar. Rather, she devours the blossom with all her senses: inhaling the fragrance, savoring the taste, absorbing the color. She imbibes the song of joy evoked by sunlight on petals. Back in the hive, she also shares her bounty with the community. As they gather in a circle, each bee dances an expression of the blessings she has gathered: dancing the joy, dancing the splendor, dancing the delight. One by one, they add their share to fill the cauldron in the center. Then all dance together, encircling the cauldron, singing the praises of the visible face of the spirits. The resulting blend will ripen and ferment into a honey that is also rich and sweet—and to most people utterly invisible. As a walker on our Path of Pollen you may seek out this honey—it is your right as the Bee Master's final student—and if found and imbibed, one single drop will change you forever.

"*The Melissae are thus as two groups of three sisters. Mythically, they are as the northern Fates, the Norns, the Wyrd sisters. The Melissae carry a function of priestess and produce sweet elixirs that ensure fertility, at the same time retaining autonomy and control over their sexuality and sexual reproduction. This includes control of the flow of their moon-juices.*

"*You are aware that to our forebears, honey was deemed to be divine. The priestesses of Eleusis were known as Melissae, and their temple was known as the beehive. Within the Path of Pollen, the temple, the beehive, denotes a Melissa's body. The honeycomb signifies that which is interior to the physical, the alchemical body, in which is created the choicest nektars* and aromas of earthly experience. The bee and the Melissae carry into the hive what lives in the flower. If you reflect on this, you will unlock the secret we carry. The living element of this sexual power that is spread all over the flower is also contained within the honey the bee creates. What does this honey do? It creates sensual pleasure, upon the tongue in particular, and when imbibed, it creates a circuit of force between sexual power, mind, and emotion. Furthermore, because the bee is influenced most of all by cosmic forces, by communing with the bee, the entire cosmos can find its way into human beings, assisting them in stepping into who they truly are, before they were told who they were meant to be by their parents, their schooling, their culture.*

---

*Nektars with a *k* are those produced by the Melissae, and are distinguished from *nectar* with a c, which is produced by the flower.

"The nektars are very singular fluids. They are produced from the bodies of the Melissae—and let us remember that when we eat honey from the bee, we are eating a very sweet and pure form of vomit, for the nectar collected into the stomach of the bee is then regurgitated. The nektars created by the Melissae are a spiritual honey. Just as the bee has inscribed on its tongue, in its mouth, and in its stomach that it is to make honey, so it is inscribed in our eyes, ears, marrow, and wombs that we transform that which we absorb from certain things of the earth into certain types of spiritual honey—the nektars. We are intended and impelled to produce these precious fluids. The Melissae respond to this incomprehensible calling.

"The Melissae work with their interior stars, each of which is aligned to certain exterior stars, as well as to specific glands within the body: pineal, pituitary, thyroid, parathyroid, thymus, pancreatic, adrenal, and sexual. Their work is to produce nektars. These nektars are produced when a Melissa becomes as a flower; she is One Who Flows—the flow-er. There are ten nektars, embodying the formula of nine plus one. The final nektar—the tenth—is invisible and must be arrived at only if the initiate is ready to imbibe it, for if he is not, it becomes a venom and may bring about his death."

If I understood correctly, the Bee Mistress was saying that these nektars were—are—a form of psycho-cosmic fluids created and distilled in the laboratories that are the bodies of the Melissae. The Bee Mistress went on to explain that each of the nektars carries a different ambience, application, and impact. She referred to them as the Ten Nektars of the Flower. The first was urine: Nektar of Golden Rain, whose symbol was the downward-facing triangle bisected by a lightning flash. Upon asking for an example of how this might be used, she went silent, seemingly pondering what would be a suitable example to offer. She eventually responded, stating that by "making water" on the body of a woman who represents Earth, rainfall could be achieved. "But this is an elementary usage of this nektar," she added, "a limbering-up exercise, you might say." She went on to explain that it was considered the weakest of all the nektars in terms of its potency and application.

The second sacred secretion, menstrual blood, was named Nektar of Moon Dew and carried the symbol of the vesica piscis. "Our wisdom is not clear and thin like water, but thick and dark like our moon blood," intoned the Bee Mistress. An overview of the other nektars—unguents, treacles, dews, juices, emanations, and rays—followed, each of which, I understood, carried its own symbol system, colors, and rituals of activation and transmission. The tenth nektar, whose symbol was the three-dimensional lemnisicate, was nameless, ineffable. "Thus," said the Bee Mistress, "as the bee carries on the work for which she is appointed—the pollination of herb and tree blossom and the provision of surplus honey for humankind—so the Melissae pollinate in a different manner and bring honey for their own."

As the story of the Melissae further unfolded, I learned that these enchanting women moved around a three-aspected system of Sisterhoods that existed within the Sisterhood of the Hive. The first is the Sisterhood of the Spinners. Its members concentrate on the arts and crafts. It is here that the Melissae learn how to build the hive, how to make and shape hives and verses, hearths, homes, and creativity. They also learn the art of the spinner—the ancient art of the spider weaving a thread or a cloth to represent the lives of men—learning how to spin webs of victory and destiny. They are cunning and industrious. At times, they have the power to weave a man's fate and even his death, as was indicated in the chant the Bee Mistress gently sang:

> *Fair weft and fitting warp,*
> *Weave a web that bids life forth.*
> *Fair warp and fitting weft,*
> *Weave a web that calls to death.*

"You can concentrate the history of the Spinners into the evolution of flax, cotton, and wool fiber," she added, before telling me of one of the Melissae who worked with oracles and divination, a tradition that comes from Delphi, where the oracle was revealed by a swarm of bees. In fact, the *pythia*, or divinatory, mantic priestesses, in Delphi's temple of Apollo were affectionately called Delphic bees.

The second sisterhood is the Sisterhood of Wise Maidens. These women are taught the principles behind a woman's life and work and are instructed in the medicinal skills associated with the hive. They are also taught the Seven Secret Songs of the hive, how to synthesize the message of the tradition, and how to master the art of storytelling—not as a pastime, but as a magic, wherein the tales truly come to life, allowing the listeners to step into the stories' landscapes.

The third sisterhood is the Sisterhood of the Fays, or faery women. These are not denizens of elf-land, but rather human women who have become mistresses of the magical arts and of the wisdom that lies behind these arts. The Melissae of this sisterhood have been initiated into the principles behind magical mating and the arts of shape-shifting and flight. They are the mistresses of sexuality and thus possess the ability to choose whether to be impregnated. This arcane art that controls whether the sperm meets an egg is one small part of their mysteries.

The Bee Mistress finished her instruction and picked up a small bell on her sideboard, ringing it gently. With absolute silence a door opened and two of the Melissae entered, wearing their ceremonial vestments but without their veils. They were Vivienne and Devorah, whom I correctly assumed were the senior Melissae, representing the magnetic and maternal aspects, respectively.

The Bee Mistress introduced us. "This is the Bee Master's charge," she began, "and these are my senior Melissae, Devorah and Vivienne. They are here to see what is held for you, and for me to see what your inclination is toward type. Devorah* will step

---

* The names taken by the Melissae were chosen with great care. Devorah, which in the modern world is usually pronounced as and spelled Deborah, comes from the Hebrew word for bee, *dbvrh*, which itself has its origins in the verb *d.b.r.* meaning speech. As this was a woman who used language as her magic, it was an eminently well-chosen name for this Melissa.

into her rank and duty as pythia and oracle, and Vivienne will seek the strengths and weaknesses of your abilities with vertical and horizontal polarity and your ability to create the circuit of force."

At that, the Bee Mistress rose and left her quarters, leaving the three of us standing: myself—awkward and uncomfortable, lost as to what to say—in strong contrast to the Melissae's quiet confidence. Indeed, it was clear that they were not about to speak. I recalled what Bridge had said on this matter: "Language transmits the thought of the speaker, but we cannot grasp the subtle meaning of words unless we drop all preconceived ideas and listen without referring to our own opinions, which veil comprehension. Thus, silence is often the better medium for communing." He had gone on to say that at every instant, each thought and gesture modifies the invisible weft upon which the Fates weave patterns of our destiny, which we, knowingly or unknowingly, prepare.

I looked at them and attempted a friendly smile, which came out as a quizzical, bewildered look. It was ignored. Did they know I had no idea what to expect? Perhaps they thought I was an expert, or at least had been tutored, on whatever was to follow. I tried to breathe slowly and deeply to calm myself and attempted to take them in. Breathe in. Breathe out.

Devorah—who had collected one of the masks from the wall*, a witch-hag image with a large, hooked nose and two

---

* The ritual masks used within the Path of Pollen—all carved from a single block of wood—are always hung facing the wall when they are not being used or being readied for use.

flapping tongues—had begun to unfold a bundle the size of a newborn child onto a small table. She was of pale complexion, with glittering golden hair. Clearly dressed for ceremony, she wore a small coronet on her head from which flowed a veil of golden cloth. Her dress was black but ornamented with gold lace, her head delicately shaped as though it had been modeled by an artist, her nose small and slightly aquiline, her forehead so full and open that it lent a virile quality to her face. Her whole person was in prefect proportion but inclined to slenderness, relieved by full hips that were emphasized by their strong, easy swing when she moved around the table that she was preparing.

Vivienne was altogether different. Dark-skinned and with beautiful features, she was a true daughter of Egypt, with an oval face and rebellious, raven black hair that seemed to writhe like the serpent locks of Medusa. But everything else faded into insignificance when it came to her deeply set eyes, for they had a glamour and a mysterious wildness that beckoned me and filled me with an impossible yearning. Her eyebrows were so thick that they seemed to form an uninterrupted line across her face, the effect of which was simultaneously sinister and fascinating. She stood silently, a female herm, alternately watching her sister Melissa and glancing toward me, wearing her intensity as a garment.

And then she moved across to the opposite end of the room, sliding behind the loom so that she was partially out of view. In her movements she was a panther, and every action was brusque, as though she were driven to seize an impulse. She opened a cupboard and removed what appeared to be the skin of a large stag; she brought it over to Devorah and hung it over a three-legged stool that Devorah then sat on. Even the curve of her wrist as she placed the skin across the stool was full of a natural grace.

Vivienne then turned and came toward me, stopping at arm's length where our shadows met. She abruptly closed her eyes and, in contrast with her brusque movements of moments before, she unfurled the layers of herself, falling like goose down from her head to her toes. I stole a glance toward Devorah as she placed resins onto a piece of burning charcoal that she had removed from the hearth fire and placed within a small earthenware thurible. She began to move her hands in a circular motion through the thick smoke that rose to meet her, as if beckoning forth an invisible world, and then placed her head low, plunging her face into the wall of rising smoke, inhaling deeply.

I moved my attention back to Vivienne and studied her. With closed eyes, now moving rapidly beneath her lids, I felt I was gazing on a mystery. Slowly her eyelids opened and her eyes—burning with a luminous serenity—met mine. She tilted her neck back slightly and opened her mouth, indicating that she had pinned her tongue to its roof and that I should do the same. As I held my tongue to my palate, I felt my nervousness melt as she emanated a soothing, mesmeric current of sound. I was soon to know that these eyes could move from soothing serenity to flashing sparks from their jet blackness as she became aroused, but now she silently took me into quietude and began to sway gently, her waist and her breathing conjoined in rhythm as she inhaled deeply into her lower abdomen, working her lungs like a bellows. The mystic rite had begun.

After a few moments she brought her arms and hands upward, bending them at the elbows, and she joined both palms together in front of her as if in prayer. She traced the outline of a large hourglass figure of infinity, circling over her head and down below her waist, the pattern crossing over itself at the level of her heart. As she executed this curious pass in the air, it was as if something or someone was turning up a wick within her; she became brighter and brighter by the moment. Each pass contained one full breath, with her inhaling on its ascent and exhaling on its declension. Her arms were a serpent climbing and twisting through the branches of a tree.

Her body swaying, she began to trace a diamond shape with her feet, while through it all she stared at me, unblinking. I was meant to meet her in these movements, that much I knew, and so I responded by mimicking her, badly and awkwardly at first but slowly with a greater fluency. Eventually, as I had established the rhythm, she released her palms from each other and held them across to me, right hand crossed over left, with palms and arms outstretched. Again I mirrored her, so that my palms met hers. I saw then that our bodily movements each represented one half of the *leminiscus infinitorum*, and that now, with our hands touching like the old hand-fasting ritual of marriage, we were once again repeating the symbol. But what graphic cycle of infinity, what perichoretic dance was being played out?

Devorah, now masked, had begun to tap her feet in a slow, monotonous tempo, and in response to this, Vivienne began to circumambulate. I followed her, and together we formed the outline of a circle with our feet, the smoke from the thurible beginning to collect around us. Moment by moment, Devorah's tapping on the floor gradually increased in tempo and harshness, and our movements became entrained by this. Still we held on to each other, twin circles conjoined in a rolling circumgyration. As our speed increased, we swung with a greater momentum, around and around, as if we were re-creating a children's game or a traditional folk dance, but the trajectory of this dance lay beyond the playground or dance hall.

I saw in my peripheral vision Devorah, the pythoness, sitting on her throne of skins, her body swaying with a curious quivering movement of the hips as though a sigmoidal force was beginning to possess her. Her golden tresses fell in masses over her face as she uttered rasping sounds and dark laughter in guttural, otherworldly voices, as if she were a serpent who had to sing. The strictures of the mask gave her the appearance of having two streams of blood pouring from her mouth.

But it was Vivienne's eyes—as dark as a thunderstorm—that snapped back my attention. There was now a terrible magnetic force in her dancing, as if a part of her were sinking under the brutal possession of a dark god, her body insisting on faster and faster speeds of turning as the sound of Devorah's feet became a thump and then a stomp accompanied by the roar of sound in my head from my own frantic heartbeat. On and on it went, and all the while we were relentlessly whirling in a rotary motion, revolution after revolution. Sweat poured down my face and a glorious, heady freedom began to thrum in my veins. Vivienne's eyes held me in a grip that was as viselike as the grasp of her hands, and the effort involved in the work receded as if we now had our own traction.

And then I saw the awful and the terrible and the beautiful: Her mouth began to change and grow in shape, to extend grossly. Her lips sealed over and a preternatural tongue—an extended proboscis—emerged from this closed fissure and stretched out to me. I saw, too, that a proboscis had begun to form from my own mouth, the one searching for the other like blind worms. They met as fleshy trumpets, and a furious, noisy taking and giving of fluids ensued between the two creatures, like barbarous twin hummingbirds. I was fed sweet fluids—a nektar, a fuel, but of what strange god?

Light whirled in front of my eyes as if the taste of the nektar needed to find relief within another sense, it being too much for taste alone. And in this gorging I knew her outer petals and her inner sepals, and I felt myself as a bee sinking into the sanctum of a bloom. I felt her heartbeat against my chest, throbbing as if it were an engine that made the planet turn, she and I bound together forcefully as distant words from the Bee Master crossed the vastness of my emptied mind: "The calyx is the bride-chamber in which the stamen and pistil solemnize their nuptials."

And in all of this honey-lust we continued to whirl, being

pulled into ever tighter circles. Still faster we moved, swirling and rocketing through and into the dervish of matter, the physical world around us collapsing in unholy chaos like a colossal decaying termite mound, and the room was a blurred snowstorm of corporeality and matter.

The stamping of feet stopped. What little light there had been was gone. We were surrounded by stars and silence. Unseparated twisting was all that remained.

It was cold. We were in flight—in dark orbit—outside of time, hurled within a cosmic pattern of the infinite, moving from Earth to other planets, to abodes in the stars. I lost my grip and fell away. I opened my mouth to scream but my scream was silent. A rope appeared to pull me across the gap that separated us, and as I grabbed it and was yanked toward her, I saw the rope was a flesh-vine emanating from her belly.

My extended tongue dared to enter the chalice of the flower. It slid forward and stretched to the utmost so as to reach the sublime essence, invisible nektar, and at the same time the sides of my tongue folded toward its center along its entire length so that it became a tube through which liquid could be drawn up. We were an alchemical expression—a human laboratory of cauldron and furnace. We were traveling a whirling track, a funnel that we moved within and that moved within us, and with this stretching of the lemniscate came the distortion of sound and vibration, as if sound itself had become contorted as we moved at incomprehensible speeds toward infinity itself.

My interior stars polarized with planets in the sweeping pattern of infinity, connected like the strings of a celestial harp. Visible harmonics created a music of the spheres, conjoining the single human with the living planets of our solar system, each one informing me, feeding me, strengthening me.

We continued to spin with an impossible speed, the pressure, weight, and bulk of infinity hammering at my head, and I knew that she was pulling me into the sun as a climax to this nuptial flight. Human shape had left us. Fleshy ovary pouches containing seeds were all that was left—a stigma with a glutinous coating, bags of pollen mounted on stalks clustering around a central style. I did not know how long I could bear this scorching heat or if she would grant me sweet release. But then I felt her body tighten like a fist. Anticipation wound like a spring inside me, tighter and tighter, pounding. The anticipation exploded into a firestorm of sensation. We shuddered together climactically and at that moment merged and erupted with ecstasy, as waves of golden light issued from her Gate of Life. A blinding light of exploding suns accompanied this outpouring, and we were at the heart of eternity while time roared off.

I collapsed, still spinning. Vivienne lay limp, damp, and lifeless beneath me. The holy seizure was over, the ritual enactment of the universal essence complete. I lay still, unable to move, internally staggered by what had happened. *I have a body,* I remembered.

The fire in the corner had burned low and the night had

changed; all that remained was a drifting cloud of incense. Through this dark haze of smoke I saw the Bee Mistress enter the room. She looked briefly at Vivienne and myself and then toward Devorah, with a minute nod as a question mark. Devorah replied with a single vatic utterance: "Emissary."

7

Vitamin Pan

O Goat-Foot God of Arcady!
This modern world hath need of thee!
OSCAR WILDE, "PAN"

It was an overcast, drizzling day at Monks Bench. A low-slung, monotonous gray sky had sent the bees—minions and worshippers of the sun—back to their hives. Even the lightest of rains would have them vanish.

We were comfortably installed inside the house; the wood burner was lit, gently releasing the scent of apple wood and an infusion of calm. The Bee Master sat across from me in one of the two large and well-worn chairs on either side of the hearth. It was a pristine and spartan room that oozed an abundant and nourishing energy, the exact source of which was impossible to locate. Frivolity was present nowhere in this house, but the simple richness of a space where everything had purpose made it perpetually fulfilling to be present there.

Bridge casually mentioned that it was now time for him to explain the making of a particular tool that was used by the male practitioners within the Path of Pollen. I imagined it would be some form of instrument for working with the bees, like the smoker perhaps, or the tanging quoit—a specialist tool for the master of the arts.

Bridge, as usual having direct access to my thoughts, smiled sympathetically and replied that yes, in a manner of speaking the tool was indeed used for working with the bees, but less directly than those I had been introduced to until then.

"The tool that you will be making, Twig, is known to us as the Ancestral Rick.* *The Bee Master knows* the Ancestral Rick is the symbolic re-creation of the tail of the first Bee Master, a being known to us simply as the Sorcerer."

"The first Bee Master had a tail?" I interjected with barely contained astonishment, bordering on disbelief. "And why was he called a sorcerer?" I added. "Isn't that a derogatory term?"

Bridge paused, perhaps struck by my sudden brow-lifted look of surprise, or perhaps with some small apprehension at continuing with his lecture. This caused an uncomfortable seed of unease to take root in me and I found myself starting to fidget.

"*The Bee Master knows* that the Sorcerer had such an overwhelming affection for the honeybee that he actually changed his shape, his physical human form, taking on certain physical characteristics of a stag, much like ecstatic Christians might experi-

---

* The women on the Path of Pollen work with a different tool, the Ancestral Bundle, which is based on similar principles. It is hoped that this will be detailed by one of the Melissae in due time.

ence stigmata due to the depth and intensity of their devotion. And why a stag in particular? The Sorcerer *knew*, as all Bee Masters know, that the stag was the representative beast of the great god Pan, the horned and hoofed nature deity. You will recall what you have been told of the vitamin that comes when in contact with pollen—vitamin P? Well, as many of the older books on bee-keeping record, Pan—a half-goat, half-man—was and continues to be the protector of the bees. This is how we know him."

He slid an old book from his bookcase and opened it to a line drawing of a horned, priapic goat-man. Beneath it lay a Latin inscription, which he translated: "Having left the slopes of Maenalus, I abide here to guard the hives, on the watch for him who steals the bees." He then pulled out a small silver coin from his pocket and flipped it over to me. I caught and inspected it; on one side was depicted a bee and on the other a stag. "The bee and the stag, Twig; conjoined and coined in Greece some two thousand years ago; the stag and the bee, conjoined then as now.*

"Reflect, Twig, that if the primary symbol of the bee is the lemniscate, the primary symbol of the stag is the circle with the semicircle above it, the symbol astrologers use for the sign of Taurus, the bull. Looked at another way, this symbol of the stag is a lem-

---

* This coin, now in my possession, has been dated between 370 and 340 B.C.E. and originates from Ephesus, which was founded by Ionian colonists and was captured by Croesus, King of Lydia. Croesus was largely responsible for the construction there of a great temple to the goddess Artemis, whose priestesses were—of course—the Melissae. Similar coins depicting the implied symbiotic relationship between bee and stag can be found in museums the world over.

niscate, but open to the heavens above. *The Bee Master knows* that the horns of a stag mediate from above and radiate primal sentient life; it is a leminiscate, partly hidden in its communion with life.

"And so, as part of our work, we reach out to the protector of the bees, and we do this by making our Ancestral Rick, to commune with the Sorcerer and through him with Pan, the Horned One, the Lord of the Hunt. The Sorcerer—as *we* use the term—went back to the *source* to do his work, and in this we become the Sorcerer connecting us to what the Welsh bard Dylan Thomas knew of as the 'force that through the green fuse drives the flower.' "

Bridge then outlined the methodology of making the Ancestral Rick: I was to collect a number of sticks—twigs—each one a symbolic depiction of my tutelary spirits or spiritual allies. Typically these were of human or animal form, but they might also appear as plants, stones, clouds, or any other of nature's manifestations. In locating these sticks I was to follow a very specific protocol and undertake a series of walks, walks of vigilance. This involved my holding a clear intent to locate the appropriate twig, or, rather, to allow myself to be found by the twig, having sent out my silent request through the fringes of nature to this quarry that would then reveal itself to me. This was a common thread in all the work of nature—that nature herself signals to you if a resource was needed, whether a stone, an animal, even an element. Over the next few months, I gradually collected a bundle of sticks, each one embodying a connection and relationship to my spiritual teachers.

One of the sticks represented Herr Professor. It came to me as his words had done at pertinent moments over the years and opened up a path inside me. "Nothing to fear," he would whisper. The volume and wave of his words would surround me, engulf me, and on this occasion, as the surge arrived, so too did the twig. Other sticks represented places in nature that nurtured me, places in nature where I was able to discover something of my own nature. There were also sticks relating to the bees, to the hive. Each one had been carefully chosen and found its way to me.

The next stage was to mark each twig to ensure that I could specifically identify it once they were all bound together. This was done with combinations of colored thread, carving, and pyrography.

I was then told of the next stage of the work. I was to collect a small amount of emanations from my body: hair from different parts of my body, nail clippings, mucus, tears, semen, blood, and sweat—everything except for feces. These would then be rolled together into a small, tight ball and placed in a pouch, which was to be made from the scrotum of a stag. This pouch was then to be placed in the center of my bundle of twigs, which would be bound together at both ends so that I would be left with something that would look akin to the bushy end of a witch's broom—a broom with no handle.

I would then be both symbolically and energetically surrounded by my allies and my ancestors, at the center of what Bridge referred to as my Circle of Reality. Once this had been achieved, I would learn to feed this tool with pollen, and in time the Ancestral Rick would begin to reveal to me how it wished to be utilized. This all seemed straightforward enough.

What came next, however, hit me directly behind the knees, and the internal balance I was finding with this new task was immediately gone. The stag I would have to hunt and kill—slaughter—myself. As if that were not challenge enough, what followed was astounding: The stag would have to be killed not by a bullet or even an arrow, but rather with my bare hands. I would need to suffocate the creature *with pollen*.

"Your task will be to capture the deer, specifically a male red deer. The stag instinctively travels in wide circles and it is his nature to graze frequently. By constantly keeping him on the move, you will succeed in tiring him and then driving him to exhaustion." My incredulity ballooned, but Bridge continued the Knowledge Lecture at a brisk march. He would not indulge me, and he completely disregarded my horror.

"If you do your job well, you will have guided him into an area where you will have raised a net, and having exhausted the buck and entangled it in the net, you will run toward it with all your might, pushing all your weight against its side and taking it to the ground. While it is on the ground, you will hold it by the neck, and at the same time you will grab the pollen you will be carrying in two bags around your waist, one to your right and another to your left; your bidextrous skills will be to your advantage here and during the hunt." I was to press the pollen firmly against the mouth and nose of the deer. I was to hold it until the deer stopped breathing and stopped moving. I was then to remove the scrotum and gut the deer in accordance with precise instructions that would be forthcoming.

These words slip onto the page with ease, it now being some years after the event. But as someone who had been a vegetarian from the age of eleven to my mid-twenties, living off yogurt, fruits, and vegetables, who was a lover of animals, and who had encountered animals in the wild with Herr Professor, the task of killing a deer was near repugnant to me. It also sounded near impossible. Yes, I knew of the red deer—I knew that it was Britain's largest native land mammal—but how was I to capture it with a net? It sounded preposterous. Moreover, should I succeed in netting the great beast, would I be capable of killing it in cold blood?

But Bridge was blunt on the matter: It was the next gateway of my training and I could go no further until this had been completed. He said it would make greater sense once the hunt was over. But when I left Bridge's company that day, I considered for the first time that I might have to abandon this path. There seemed an incongruence between my beliefs and his, with two primary dilemmas, the moralistic and the humanistic.

That night I climbed into my heathen hammock, my dreaming web, and dreamt that I met Pan, Lord of the Animals, God of the Bees. I asked him what power he held over animals, and he replied, "Little man, I will show you." He took his cudgel and struck a bull stag with a great blow, so that it roared. It was as if the stag's head was a bell that let out a clarion call. With that, wild animals began to arrive until they were like stars in the sky, so that there was scarcely room for me to stand among the badgers, foxes, field mice, owls and falcons, adders and voles, and animals of all sorts.

The next time I saw Bridge, he continued with his talk: "This is the way it has always been done, Twig: The apprentice suffocates the deer with sacred bee pollen, and as he does this he communes with the creature, he thanks the deer for the gift of his life, and he pledges that his life will be honored by authentic actions in the world." Bridge added that using pollen would also ensure that the hide was perfect, unpierced by bullet or arrow—the type of hide always most prized for use in ceremony. I was reminded that Devorah had used the skin of a stag during the ceremony when she stepped into the role of pythia.

"Twig, if we look toward the most ancient of times, to when we most depended on meat for our own survival, our ancestors found it highly problematic to prey upon our fellow animals. So it is today, and the hunt is surrounded by ceremony and sanctions designed in part to assuage guilt and also to know and to see the posthumous existence for the beast. Killing was and is a terrible but necessary act, and the shock of sacred awe, when the stag receives the pollen, paradoxically gives us a profound sense of the sacred value of life. It also forces us to confront the violence upon which civilization depended—and still depends, although today we have a culture that carefully shields itself from this uncomfortable perception. It is possible, for example, to buy a neatly packaged joint of meat without giving a thought to the way the animal lived, or died. We must never lose our sense of the awful gravity of the procedure, because—as with those who have gone before us—therein lies our sense of life's sacred value. Twig, I know this will be a difficult task for you, lad, but through this task you will know better that death is not the negation of life. Death brings meaning to life: Our lives— our bodies—are nourished by the death of plants and animals. Be clear: Our deaths will one day serve as nourishment for them. Through their magical powers to re-create the animals on the walls of the temple caves, our ancestors connected the living with the source of the life that animated both human and animal, becoming themselves vehicles of that source, or sorcerers— creators of the living form, like the source itself.

"Hunters would usually know the habits and habitats of the animal world intimately, and they felt an almost personal bond with the animals they tracked."

I retorted that I knew none of this—I had not so much as caught a butterfly in a net. Bridge answered that this was the point, that this activity was performed from a place of innocence and vigilance, being driven from the power of the tradition of which I was now a part, that the Sorcerer himself would be present in my movements and my moods. Finally, he said that before setting out, I would seek to discover my quarry within a dream. This would be a sign that the creature would willingly surrender itself to me, an agreement between myself and the stag, an appointment that was agreed upon by both of us and would be honored.

That night I went into sleep with the intention that I would hunt the dream of the stag. I awoke in a glade and next to me lay a grand stag that I had killed. I looked at it closely and counted the points on its antlers, knowing that I would use this to recognize the stag when I met with it. I was lying next to a shallow stream as I cut open the stag and removed its heart. I took the heart to the stream to wash the blood from the meat. From a clot of blood, a boy began to grow. For the next few months I had the dream repeatedly. Each time it was the same stag that I killed and each time the heart was washed in the stream, the boy growing a little more with each dream. But however hard I tried, I could never see the boy's face.

The day arrived for me to leave for the hunt. As well as my having sparse knowledge of the stag and its habits, I also knew nothing of the terrain where the hunt would take place. This was to be an act of trust. All I knew was that we were heading north and that the drive was long. The idea of a human being taking down a stag with his bare hands still seemed absurd and dangerous. The little I did know was that the red deer had been on the British Isles for more than ten thousand years, and that since extermination of the wolf some two hundred years ago, human beings were their only predators. I was also aware that a full-grown buck can stand at least four feet in height at the shoulder and carry a large rack of antlers that would now in the early autumn be in peak condition for the rut, when they are used for sparring rituals between rivals. So the stags would be at their maximum fitness, ready to compete with others. What hope would I possibly have against such a formidable beast?

The Bee Master had given me various items to take on the hunt, including a net about thirty feet long into which the stag was to be chased. This net, Bridge informed me, had been woven by the Melissa Nivetta of the Sisterhood of the Spinners, and was made using a combination of milkweed fiber and hair. It had been dyed with walnut hulls: Their outer green shells had been collected when the nuts had fallen in the autumn, at which point they had been placed in water and stored there over the winter months. Bark of alder and elder together with roots of sorrel and dandelion were used as supplementary dyes. I was also given a tube that looked like a bagpipe chanter, which held a reed at one end and when blown down would make the sound of the stag's grunt, much like the way a duck call is used. This, Bridge stated, should be used only if I was unable to locate my stag by stealth and stalking. I had sufficient food for about ten days in the form of a large jar of pollen and another one of honey on the comb. Beyond that, I carried a small saucepan for making tea, a handful of tea bags, some matches, and sections of board and some ropes to construct two makeshift stands, miniature tree houses with neither roof nor walls, their purpose being as lookout posts. I also had a hunting knife and a flask for water.

Bridge handed me a small pendant hung on an old piece of twine, which The pendant carried an image of a bee in flight carved into the Welsh slate. The Bee Master told me to wear it once I met with the stag, saying that this fetish—which had been worn by previous apprentices as they stepped out on this quest—contained the quality of the bee's tenacity, which would keep the buck anxious and on the move.

"Now you see why I have been getting you to observe the flight of the bee," he added. It was true; the discipline of following the flight of a single bee from hive to flower and back had made me fitter than I had been as a young and athletic teenager. Bees can travel up to twenty miles an hour and are happy to fly over several miles as part of their foraging work. On more than one occasion, I had heard Bridge's distinctive cackle as he watched me get caught up in brambles and trip over stiles in my attempt to keep pace with a tiny gold-and-amber pinion with wings beating sixteen thousand times a minute. Over time, I had learned to move swiftly and with incredible agility, but would this give me the speed and strength to run down a deer?

He also said that challenge and adventure brought the chance to meet with the tonic that modern people so badly needed: "Vitamin P, Twig, vitamin P! This is what my teacher called it: vitamin Pan, 'half a goat and half a man,' " he sang from the old chant. I was to commune with the spirit of Pan to develop a symbiotic relationship with him. Thus the prey I would be seeking would in the meantime become my teacher. Finally, Bridge took out a vial of liquid and told me that when the time was close, I should put several droplets in my eyes. He would say no more on the matter.

Bridge spoke his parting words to me: *"The Bee Master knows the stags are ghostlike in their effortless movements. The way to hunt the stag is to become as a ghost yourself."*

When I stepped into the woods, there was a sense of belonging. The air was pure and the silence refreshing. It was private and unvisited. The dense canopy allowed little direct sunlight to reach the woodland floor. I made a small camp in the only stretch of open woodland I could find, where yew trees took second place to towering conifers, trembling ash, and majestic oak. I reckoned that this was as good a place as any to set up camp, but as far as I could tell, there were no signs of stag activity. Where was he?

I spent the next three days and nights exploring the woodland. It was damp and quiet, and the walking was easy. I came across travelways used by various woodland creatures and considered that I had found the stag's tracks going in both directions on one particular trail. I lay down upon the tracks and allowed my body to feel the imprints they made upon the earth. Then I covered my entire body in the soft mud and leaves from the trail, disguising my human scent.

Each night I slept under piles of fallen leaves, filling the layers of my clothing with the natural insulation of leaves, mosses, and dried ferns. And with the arrival of every dawn I felt more part of the woods and the woods more part of me. I would dream of the Horned God of the Hunt surrounded by many beasts of the forest, who would nightly present me with a golden torc that I would place about my neck.

With the dawn I would make a small fire and when the water boiled I would pop in some wild mint and brew a refreshing tea.

139

Honey was supped straight from the jar, and a mound of golden pollen grains was taken in as my main meal of the day. And then I would begin to stalk. Shafts of leveling sunlight fell between the trunks of chestnut trees, making the leaves transparent. The woodland seemed to be hiding some focal point of force that both drew and repelled me. Doubt was pressing me backward as though from a defended place. I scanned the woodland again and again for any sign of dangerous beasts, but there was none; the menace had some less tangible source.

With each day, I went farther and deeper into the woodland. By the fifth day, I had witnessed much of nature, but still nothing of the stag, although I had discovered a dim glade where deer seemed to return again and again, but never in my presence. When I first entered this place, there was a whiff of mint hanging in the still air. Had he moved silently ahead of me, crushing the wild herb that grew on the edges of the small streams that ran through the woodland?

I spent the first hours of that day erecting a primitive stand up a birch tree where I could overlook the glade. I climbed up the tree and began my vigil. Completely still, I sat watching.

For two days and nights, I sat cross-legged in this stand from the moment sunlight would first trickle down the tree trunk until darkness would make my hand in front of my face invisible to me, all the time sinking deeper into the woodland and my relationship with her tenants. Partridge patrolled the forest floor; squirrels scurried up trunks with fruit and nuts the size of their head and crammed them between forks in the tree limbs lest others gobble them up. And then there was the moment between dusk and nightfall, the betwixt and between, when time itself would stop.

Despite the beauty around me, by the third day I was wet, cold, and discouraged, and I had seen nothing of the stag. I had left my stand only twice, to drink and to cover myself again in scents of the forest. Low clouds that seemed full of ink surrounded me, dusk was on its way, and I was reflecting on where I would be resting my head that night. I pulled my attention back to my task and allowed to arrive on my tongue a chant, which I began to sing so softly that it was barely audible even to me.

> *Comes the stag to my singing,*
> *Comes the stag to my song,*
> *Comes the deer to my singing.*
> *From the heart of the wood,*
> *Through the bush and the blossom,*
> *Comes the stag to my singing.*
> *Coming now to my singing,*
> *Coming now to my song,*
> *Comes the stag to my singing. . .*

Suddenly, a deer crashed out of the thick brush and headed right toward my tree. I could see it was the buck from my dream. He stopped a few feet from the bottom of the tree, raising his head high and smelling the currents. The great stag then lay and rolled, cooling his body in the black mud, away from any eyes except those of the wilderness. Then, as suddenly as he had appeared, he was gone. My heart pounding, I climbed down from my stand, knowing without doubt that this was the beast with whom I had an appointment. The smell of the male deer was present in the air and a tremor ran through me that tempted me to action, but I also sensed that our time had not quite arrived. I placed the pendant around my neck in readiness, lifted it to my lips and breathed it in, hoping that in this inhaling, some of its essence that Bridge said it contained would be imbued within me.

I had discovered a small lake—in truth, little more than a large puddle, but it held an atmosphere that was close to that of my dream of the fallen stag. The boundaries of this still space barely segregated water and earth as the sun went down, and was a watering hole for the full bestiary of the woodland. It was at one section of this watering hole that I determined to erect my net.

I slept then, arising before dawn. My night had been laden with dreams that could not—would not—cloak either my fear of failure or the abject terror that had been artfully obscured behind my ruthless dedication to my task. I had felt the breath of impending annihilation and attempted with iron will to force from my mind the abhorrent prospect of the actions I was to attempt. I took no tea, just a mouthful of golden ambrosia and Golden Coins, and I was off, moving swiftly and silently into the shadows.

My ears pricked up. In the distance I could just hear the roar of competing stags, sounding like a pride of lions. I moved through the undergrowth silently. If it were not for the occasional leaf crackle, I would have been mistaken for a shadow.

By now, with the dawn arriving, dark shadows were turning into trees and woods emerged from the pitch-black. As each hour passed, I learned better how to remain motionless yet completely alert amid the silent, subtle circus of activity around me. I waited and watched, ever extending the time that I remained without movement. A stillness that was beyond quiet hummed in my ears.

I began to sense that *something* was close. The faint crack of a branch to my left became the movement of a shadow. I tracked it with my eyes but not my head, and then crept closer to its source, a steady rain masking my approach. And then, there he was, the magnificent stag, stepping out of the thick brush. He seemed to look directly at me, his head inclined toward me, testing the wind with his snout and then raising his head high to assess me from a higher perspective, his neck a tower, cut from the stone of pride.

I was still, lost in the brush, the only sound my heart pounding in my chest. The stag shook off the rain from his coat and moved toward me, smelling the wind.

A magpie perched in an alder tree just above me seemed to be watching my every move and relaying it to the stag. I slowly stood up, allowing the stag to see me more clearly; it was time we met. A mere sixty feet separated us. Our eyes locked and a flurry of recognition passed between us. Simultaneously we bellowed at one another and I ran toward him, shouting of my task and of our appointment. He flinched just slightly—was he the hunted or the hunter?—and then turned on his haunches. He was gone.

I erected my net across a wide entrance to the watering hole. Then I readied myself to find the bull once again. I knew instinctively that the time had arrived for me to open the small vial of liquid that Bridge had made for me. I still did not know what it was, this mysterious liquid, but I knew instinctively that now was the time to use it, just as Bridge had said I would. As I removed the stopper, the smell of chlorophyll rose up. I tipped my head back and kept my eyes open as I dripped several droplets into each eye. It was brutally painful. After a minute of silently cursing and contorting my body, the pain eased and I looked around once again. The liquid had no doubt affected and altered my vision, for the dense green walls of the undergrowth now had a greater texture and dimension; everything seemed to both collect more light and absorb more shadow. "This will make it easier for you to find your prey," Bridge had said. I returned to the hunt.

Within an hour, despite his passion, I had located the stag once more, and I began my primal strategy. I was ruthless and would not allow him to rest. As day slipped into night, the dance of predator and prey continued. I knew that the time was close; the deer was suffering fatigue, but fear was driving him on as I ran, screaming, behind him. The stag, fueled by his wildness, his fear, and his fight for life, would not easily give way. Many times I felt he was failing, but then he would burst forth once more, driven by his hunger to live, for Pan was within him, too. This fleet-footed beast was as strong as the howling Scottish winds and resilient as the heather flourishing in its wake.

On and on we went, around and across the map of the woodland I now knew as well as the stag. I had become the hollow bone—my intellect pushed far beyond myself and beyond these woods. I ran and jumped effortlessly, with the accuracy of a mountain goat and the swiftness of a hare. It seemed I had become the hunter's arrow, shot from the bow of my unwavering intent. I was primed and ready to kill. I released the moral order that I had carried since childhood, and my heart now beat to the primal drum, signaling that hunter and hunted were hide from the same beast and death was the drummer to both.

My intuition told me that the exhausted deer would head for water as a means of cooling down and to better defend himself. I had erected my net with this very thought in mind, and now we were closing in on the pool. I felt sustained by two forces: that mysterious wisdom that guides the colony of the bees and that urgent force that brings panic in its wake to those who know not the power coiled within their loins.

The stag arrived at the stream as the Sorcerer's blood arrived in my veins. The moment had come. I ran, screaming my prayer to Pan as I flew toward the stag.

With exploding hoofs and leaves and dirt flying, the buck

lunged toward me. But then, inexplicably, he wheeled around. In silent acknowledgment, with a look back in my direction, the stag crashed into the net. At first he ran straight ahead and deeper into the mesh, but then he turned upon himself to reverse his flight and bolt away from the alien and unexpected trap.

What happened next was in slow motion; all sounds around us ceased.

The strength of the hive was with me. With all my concentration on the singular event to come, I ran toward the stag. At this, he changed direction once again, running headlong into the net. With all my might I ran into his side to topple him to the ground, as I had been told to do. At the exact moment of impact, however, the stag turned his enormous head toward mine and we collided, head to head, with incredible force. I was knocked unconscious by the blow.

I came to, my face covered in a warm, sticky pool of blood—my blood, which continued to pour from my upper lip, which I realized had been smashed open. A sharp pain came from my right thigh and I felt down my leg to find my trousers ripped open, exposing a deep and bleeding cut. I was lying next to the stag, who I momentarily thought to be dead. But no, he was still breathing. By some act of luck, serendipity, or destiny the stag had also been knocked unconscious, his head having hit the trunk of a tree when I knocked into him.

I knew that I had only moments to complete my task before the stag regained consciousness. I knelt before him to give my prayers, my thanks, but I could not speak. I felt consumed with fire and regret. I sprinkled myself with the blood from the wound in the stag's scalp, which showed a flap of fatty tissue. One of the bags of pollen had torn open and the Golden Coins were strewn across the forest floor, but the other bag was still around my waist. I opened it and filled my hand with pollen. My right arm gripping the stag's head, I brought up my left hand, covered in a mass of yellow dust, forcefully against the mouth and nose of the stag, putting all of my weight against his neck.

I expected a mad thrashing as the stag fought for his life, but there was a series of shudders, his branching antlers digging into the forest floor, although even this was enough to nearly dislodge me. I continued to hold my hand jammed against his muzzle, and I began to weep as I felt his life ebb away.

I had killed. Yes, I had taken life, and for that I felt remorse. But there is a connection to the earth that is established only when we ourselves take responsibility for the spilled blood.

I climbed upon the warm body and held him, as if I were riding him to Hades. My loss of blood had made me weak, but the strength of Pan told me I would live another day at least. I fell into exhausted slumber.

With the arrival of first light, I awakened, my hair glued to my prey with congealed blood, and I tore myself from its dark shape. A black wing of sadness had descended upon me—a vast house of darkness. The gleaming sapphire of energy from the hunt had gone. I knew I must complete my task with honor and with heart.

I disentangled the netting and spent the next hours at my job: first hoisting up the deer by its hind legs with rope from the net, tying the rope around the branches of a tree. Before anything else was done, I cut through the muscles that connect the scrotum to the stag's hindquarters, severing the spermatic cord and removing the testes from the sac. I placed the scrotum safely in the half-empty bag of pollen around my waist.

This done, I faced the final task the Bee Master had charged me with regarding my woodland initiation: the slitting open of the stomach. I had little idea of what to expect, and when the contents fell to the ground, I marveled at the engine that gave this creature life. As instructed, I removed the liver and kidneys, touching each against the same part of my own body to receive their strength. I then did this with all the body parts, including the eyes, and last the heart, which I then took to the stream to wash off the blood. Each organ from the body was buried, with prayers, and the work concluded with cleansing the internal cavity with water.

Still in silence, I covered the bloodied area with leaves and gathered my few items. I lowered the stag onto my back and, with aching muscles, I carried the fallen forest prince through the woodland to where my journey had begun.

8

The Nightshade Isle

I will arise and go now,
and go to Innisfree
And a small cabin build there,
of clay and wattles made:
Nine bean-rows will I have there,
a hive for the honey-bee,
And live alone in the bee-loud glade.

W. B. YEATS,
"THE LAKE ISLE OF INNISFREE"

I was told there were few visitors to the island who had not become possessed or, at the very least, enchanted for a time.

Our approach itself was an enchantment of sorts, for once Bridge and I had clambered down into the rowboat, released the rope from its tethering post, and started to row past the harbor walls, he began to chant in rhythmic formula. I knew and trusted his voice, but the language of his song was largely unfamiliar to me, yet at once my heart began to open to its call.

"Sit at the *front* of the boat, so everything you see is new," he had told me, as if revealing a secret for an entire way of life.

O, an oidhche,

An nochd

Éiteag na h-oidhche

Guth na meala dhuit

O, an oidhche,

An nochd

Éiteag na h-oidhche

Guth na meala dhuit

O, an oidhche,

An nochd

Éiteag na h-oidhche

Guth na meala dhuit. . .

"Oh, this eve, this night, jewel of the night, voice of honey be thine . . ." He sang this over and over again, a melodic cycle, synchronized to the rise and fall of the oars into cold, inky water. I could hardly see where the black of the sky and the black of the sea changed into each other. Occasionally the salt water sprayed across me, catching my face in its deep chill, drenching me in a Keltic twilight, while overhead that other ancient enchantress, the moon, looked down through a cloudless sky, watching our slow, earnest progress.

We had left dry land just after a rainstorm, and the gray mist and clouds had already been swept away by the wind. It was before the witching hour that we had left this seaside town known as a quintessentially worn and weathered British holiday resort. During summer days, this place was replete with donkey rides along the beach, strangers lying side to side, and beach huts battered by the wind and bleached by the sun. Here one usually found saucy postcards with images of stout matrons, weedy dads, naughty boys, and buxom birds in the most compromising positions. This night, however, we were far from this facade, greeted by a different truth that delved far below the surface.

Only the lonely, tufted sand dunes witnessed our pilgrimage across the sea. The lights from the town and then the pier itself became dimmer and more distant with every stroke of oar; the shore became a smudge and the world began to fade. All that remained was the dark sea, cold and deep for all the fathoms beneath us.

I argued with myself that I should be feeling more relaxed than I was, or at least a little more at ease—for wasn't the ocean once our home, where we set out on our evolutionary path? Isn't that why the multitudes still end up on the beaches on their holidays, still longing, somewhere in their souls, to be swallowed up by the liquid embrace of the deep?

But these reflections made no difference to my demeanor, or to the tightening in my stomach. Fear, Bridge had told me, can be one of the greatest forces in life because it can allow us to perceive things in a different light. But I now craved the familiar. The Bee Master's words had struck an ominous note.

I reflected on one of Bridge's own regrets, which he expressed shortly before we left dry land, that most people did not know their own countries, the home beneath their feet. "More English folk know Sienna better than Stamford and could recognize a Tuscan pantile or an olive tree than would know a Collyweston apple or a hornbeam," he remarked.

"We have become strangers to our own land, Twig, and one of my tasks is to get you to open your eyes and see your own country with the same sense of wonder you had when you first explored the woodlands of Vienna.

"The true oddness of the English is that behind all that plodding, diligent conformity and studied, gray predictability, there hide such extraordinary secret worlds. There are two Englands: the dull one that the tourists come to see and the secret one that perfectly ordinary people have swimming around in their unconscious. The English id is populated by the creatures dreamed into being by Blake, C. S. Lewis, Tolkien, and Rutland Boughton, all of them dancing to the music of Elgar! The English have the potential to be great dreamers; indeed, their speech is the language of vision, their traditions the way of seers and elfin folk.

"Why this temperament? Perhaps the secret lies in the mists of the climate, or the hills and the hollows of our island home; whatever the reason, this is a land of monuments and the great gestures of nature: ancient oaks, stone crosses, rolling fields, illuminated manuscripts, breaking waves, sleeping giants, milk and honey. It is these you must awaken to."

And so here I was, pulling on the oars as though I were some sort of ancient mariner on my way to visit a sacred satellite off Blake's blessed Albion. If only, he once urged, we could live like pirates, grabbing life's treasures and sailing forward on the high seas, we might honor the gift that was our life.

The row itself was exhausting and took several long hours against what felt to my inexperienced arms like hellishly demanding currents. But the sound of Bridge's voice, caught in a chant that never ceased, and the lullaby whisper of oar through water, began to weave a dream within me: of the island I would soon reach, of my own place in the world, and of the challenges to come.

I knew little about our destination and even less about the work undertaken there by the holders of hive wisdom. That would apparently be uncovered once we arrived. Bridge had, however, told me that I would need my Ancestral Rick. He further informed me that our island destination was twice born— that it had actually sunk and then risen again. And that, when it was born anew, it brought with it a second soul from the depths of the sea. In recognition of this, the island carried two names. You would not find these names on any map; they were passed down in sacred trust to those within the Path of Pollen.

And so this island, I came to realize, had two souls, two *locus genii*, with two distinct and separate personalities—one of them benign, illuminating and healing, the other malign, stark and potentially deadly. The Island of the Blessed was what Bridge called its "bright mirror"—its healing aspect—a name that for me had distant echoes of Byron and the stories of the Fortunate Isles. The Nightshade Isle was the name given to its shadow side or "dark mirror," carrying a force, a power, alien and part of an older world generally inaccessible to humans. "All islands have moods, minds, and spirits," Bridge had said. "Certain islands of power, such as this one, have temperaments that can seem almost human. Tonight, you must be alert to this island's dark soul— which is a very light sleeper and is easily roused."

But why, I asked, would anyone deliberately and willingly put himself in a place of danger? My voice revealed fear in its wavering tone compounded by an inner shudder. Why go to an island that carried such potential, if undefined, hazards? "A weak person always goes to where he is smiled at," Bridge had replied flatly.

At a certain moment, the Bee Master turned me so that I faced away from the direction of our destination and told me to close my eyes. And then, like a distant thud, I felt the presence of the island. It felt as if it were actually reaching out to me and, with a cold, silent, and reptilian glare, *inspecting* me.

Being watched, dispassionately or otherwise, by an island is hardly an everyday occurrence, and at a certain moment the level of discomfort I experienced turned from a shudder to an ache that finally overwhelmed me. As if without choice, my head jerked around; I had to look, to ingest fully what lay before me.

The island stared back and met my gaze. My stomach clenched involuntarily and I suppressed a retch. The mass of land that lay before me was dark, its dominant cliffs foreboding, holding echoes of some distant, infinitely powerful past, as if a part of sunken Lemuria had risen from its fathoms-deep grave and purposely made its way here. How could something so geographically close to Britain seem so alien?

We were forty or fifty feet from its shoreline when the current increased dramatically, the waters broken and white; there was more than a whiff of real danger. Without knowing the tides and the nuances of the rocks, only a fool would have tried to row here. From this distance the cliffs looked wild and dangerous, and the water tightened around us, the sea coming at us with fury. The boat pitched, rolled, plunged, and fluttered, the chop breaking in cold sheets across the bow, the water spraying my lips, now creamy with spit. Bridge started to bark orders to me and I responded with the trust of a child, for otherwise the panic creeping through me like a virus would have overcome me, such was the menace of the outcroppings of rock I glimpsed. We hit the shingle with a muffled crash and, gathering our bags, leapt from the boat—my last vestige of security and final link with home—and pulled it to shore. Once on the pebble- and rock-strewn surround, I noted that Bridge stood for one single moment as still as an Easter Island statue, staring out to sea. He then drew himself up, his hair wild in the moonshine, and uttered a sound that to my ears recalled tumbling waters. Then he turned and answered the question I had yet to formulate. "Always give thanks for safe passage," he said.

He turned and began to lead us slowly up the winding path of crumbling steps, bathed in silver light.

Around us I could make out bare stems of sycamores, which formed a woodland of sorts. We walked past rowan trees wearing their red berries shining like jewels in the moonlight, a moment of colored respite in our march. We walked by the remains of winter vegetation, elder, bramble, and privet—trees and shrubs that might not be handsome but were certainly vigorous. We walked past lichen-covered trees of greenish gray, whose branches threw a bluish tracery of shadow over rich tufts of grass. We walked as though on a processional, through areas where the light of the moon made the foliage look like silver filigree, and we walked in other places where the branches became shadowy, ghostly forms. There were also ravens and cormorants; it seemed the island was roofed with birds. Bridge had mentioned rare purse-web spiders and oversized slowworms. Above all the sights and sounds was a certain pungent, heavy, and overpowering scent—a heady, offensive perfume resembling human perspiration and ammonia.

"Do you care for the sweet smell of our heather, Twig?" Bridge asked enigmatically from a few paces ahead of me, with a chuckle in his voice.

The air was warm and moist and seemed to pulsate with the incomparable waves of this acrid fragrance. I was weary; it was all I could do to keep up with the Bee Master's long, purposeful strides. A steady climb eventually led us onto a barely discernible perimeter path that finally took us to an elevated plateau. It would seem that we had suddenly entered paradise. I sensed the presence of the bees before I saw them. In the distance was a series of hives set out in a large circle, some thirty feet apart from one another, with the diameter of the circle some 150 feet across. It was a welcoming but surprising sight.

We moved into the circle of hives and the scent of warm honey filled the air. From inside each of the hives came the bass-note sound of a cathedral organ, as tens of thousands of wings did the work of reducing nectar to honey. Arriving at the center of our circle, I beheld what appeared to be a small crater. I stood quietly before it and waited.

Finally Bridge spoke. "This island is our axis mundi; it is our omphalos." His tone was alarmingly reverential. "And this," he said, indicating the small crater, "is the sacred *caldera*, the center of our world, the very epicenter of those who walk the Way of the Bee." He slipped back into silence and motioned that I should make camp. He began to build a fire within the crater while I took in the fact that this—if I had understood Bridge correctly—was where the tradition had been born. I had been brought to where it all began.

I was to learn in subsequent years that transporting the bees to this island was the chief event of the year within the cultus, and it took some five or six days of work, with the exact moment of departure depending on one uncertain factor: the weather. In 1893, all but one of the hives had been lost, and two of the Melissae had drowned due to winds reaching near-unheard-of ferocity; steeple chapels across the land had been damaged or destroyed as a storm tore across England and out over the North Sea. This tragedy formed a benchmark of sorts for those upon the Path of Pollen, a dramatic event remembered in perpetuity.

The fire now roaring, Bridge opened his old leather school satchel, laying out a small cloth on the ground and spreading its contents. He removed two glass jars, a box of safety matches, a flask of water, a hunting knife, his tanging quoit, and a short arrow. He placed the larger of the two jars on the cloth; the smaller one, distinguished by a dark green stone stopper capped with black obsidian. He held it up to the light of the moon and said in an exaggerated conspiratorial whisper, "This, my lad, is why you are here. There is an old expression in the craft of the bee: ''Tis a good thing, life; but ye never really know how good till you've followed the bees to the heather'—and on this island, the bees find their special heather."

As Bridge recited this ancient saying, kneeling by the fire, watching the caress of the flames on the wood, I could almost see the expression as it would have emerged from the mouth of his own teacher, years before I was born.

Bridge held up the bottle. "This is the stuff of legend, no less! 'Tis the flying ointment of the witches."

We were now in the heart of the mystery, miles from the nearest town. But the bees were here, a million of them perhaps, singing their timeless song to the blossoming plants that stretched away on every side beneath the moon. So bathed was I in the moment that it dawned on me only slowly that the usual course of nature had been challenged, for the bees—sun-loving creatures of the day—were not in their hives slumbering, but were out beneath the full moon as if celebrating a midsummer's day. "Bridge, the bees. Why are they . . . how can they be in flight?"

"They have come to witness your dance, Twig, for they have a great part to play."

I knew a little of the history of European witchcraft and the reports of their flying ointment, and I certainly knew that it was the stuff of legend. Its use during witches' ceremonies to bring about transvection—flying by supernatural means—was an important issue in the trials of the Inquisition. As I understood it, however, there was no definitive recipe for its preparation, and if there ever had been, it had been lost in the mists of time.

Bridge lowered his tone and began to speak as the Bee Master to his charge: "*The Bee Master knows* that the flying ointment of our forebears was the jewel in the crown of ancient pharmacology. It was a poison to the layperson, but the spiritual tool sine qua non to the practitioner.

"*The Bee Master knows* that it is one of the two most revered teachings from the hive, the other being the use of the Sacramental Venom. It has been confused with all and sundry through the years, and these days it has become just another myth, a story at bedtime for the little 'uns. My own teacher named it 'sorcerers' grease'—a somewhat crude term, but then again he also talked of honey as 'bee spittle,' and"—he paused with a chuckle—"he named this sacred place Potato Island."

I could just make out that Bridge was smiling at the memory

of his salty, aweless benefactor, a Bee Master, a *sin-eater** and a man who had been an explorer of the Arctic Circle, funding the expeditions as a bee charmer performing acts of stage magic with bees.

"The formal name of this ointment within our lineage is Dark Flight. This island is where it is both created and introduced to the apprentice."

There was a brief silence, to allow me to take in what he had said, after which he continued: "Our forebears intentionally produced this psychoactive honey as a visionary tool for use in certain work. It is taken as honey, and in the form of the ritual metheglin. In fact, the bees first led our ancestors to these sacred plants. Having innocently ingested the delicious honey, those ancestors stepped into the other world and experienced ecstasy and communion with our spirit kin. After that, they followed the bees to the plants from whence this honey was made, and the beginning of the lineage was initiated. The bees called certain men and women who then sought out and forged a relationship with the hive, wishing to be part of that world as well as this.

"When did this occur?" Bridge continued. "Bees and human beings have been working together for at least four hundred thousand years. How ancient is this lineage to which you have

---

* The method of sin-eating was taught to Bridge by his teacher and was in due time passed to me. The primary duty of the sin-eater was to take upon himself the sins of a deceased person, but within the Path of Pollen the art extended itself to removing and extracting sins and illnesses from the living as well as the deceased, using methods of transmutation and transubstantiation.

been called? I cannot tell you that, Twig, but I will say that Eve's apple had not yet been eaten. I offer you the words of my teacher, who repeated them from his teacher and his before him: We are a lineage that goes back to the time when history slips into myth, and the difference between history and myth is that myth is always true.

"This island is where our dance with the bee commenced; it is the manger, the fulcrum of our tradition. The reason for this is its unique plant life, the nightside plants: *solarto* or deadly nightshade, thorn apple, and henbane all grow here, perhaps uniquely abundant in this one area of Britain." I now understood why Bridge's teacher had called this place Potato Island: These plants were all within the potato family of wildflowers of Britain and northwest Europe.* "Despite usually being found next to each other in textbooks, henbane and deadly nightshade have very different spirits, Twig. Indeed, they are like different places. Look here." Bridge pointed to a plant at my feet. "Henbane is viscid and downy to the fingers; it is the exquisite, clammy emanation of the wasteland and the sun. It calls to you from its exceedingly dark purple center and its pale, clouded, amber-yellow petals, delicately veined with purple brown. Deadly nightshade, on the other hand, is the emanation of evil in dark

---

* Deadly nightshade or belladonna (*Atropa belladonna*), thorn apple (*Datura stramonium*), and henbane (*Hyoscyamus niger*) are poisonous plants made up of potentially lethal compounds. Avoid casual experimentation with these plants because it may result in permanent brain damage, respiratory failure, or death. The link among them is atropine and atropine-like products.

corners"—Bridge motioned into the darkness—"a very suitable plant for one of the Fates—determined and strong, with wide leaves, gloom-laden flowers, and black, shining berries. Together with the third—the nectar and pollen from the large, white, trumpet-shaped flowers of the thorn apple—Dark Flight is created. You will need to make friends with the spirits of these plants, for they are our allies in this work." Bridge went on to mention that his irreverent teacher had named henbane "insane" because of its effects on certain people, and that the word *bane* was from the Old English for death. I was feeling increasingly uneasy about what might lie ahead for me.

"The traditional beekeeper might take his hives to the heather to collect his finest honey, but we bring our hives here—just the ten, but this is plenty. The bees collect the pollen and nectar from these plants, producing a honey that is the ambrosia, the quintessence of the plants, all in a concentration that has not—in living memory at least, young Twig—killed anyone. The bees are, of course, told of the aspirant who is going to be exposed to the honey for the first time, and they collect just enough of the psychotropics to bring about the necessary experience; it is their sacred prescription. A few grains of pollen, a few drops of honey is all the distance there is between one world and the other."

I was struck by the extraordinary notion that the bees produced this mythical flying ointment and did so in the exact formula to best serve the neophyte, the bees themselves performing the precise pharmaceutical and energetic opera-

tions necessary. I looked around me at the circle of hives surrounding us, each facing outward and each a whirling vortex of
life beneath the unflinching silver of the stars. I felt a curious
mixture of emotion: fear of whatever lay ahead, and privilege to
be entrusted with this information. The fire cracked and hissed
and from around me I could hear the deep chant of thousands
of bees.

"I am going to talk to you about your task tonight, and I want
you to listen well, so there are no errors." I was somewhat per-
plexed by this and it showed on my face. My mind whirled tor-
nado-like, stirring and twisting with the information I had
imbibed. Bridge smiled and said, "Confusion is often the first
stage of knowledge. What we want is *active* knowledge rather
than lazy or idle knowledge; there is far too much of that about
these days. Active knowledge can lead to wisdom, which is what
you should be aiming for. What I shall also be wanting from you
this evening is authentic action, a total act, married together with
common sense, which, truth be known, is not at all common.

"Now Twig, you are aware that after the war I traveled to
Indonesia with my teacher, to learn the ways of the Bee Masters
near Stabat on the east coast of north Sumatra. What I have not
told you is what occurred to us then. Now is the time to share
this tale, for it is an illustration of how the individual responds
to this island.

"The human being carries one primary human right and one
primary human duty. One cannot be separated from the other;
indeed, they are two sides of the human coin. The right that

should be bestowed upon all human beings is the right to do as you please. However, hand in hand with this right comes the basic human duty, which is that you must accept the consequences." As he said this, the surrounding area was suddenly engulfed in a threatening energy. In the silence, it became hard to breathe, my stomach muscles tightened, and my heartbeat became uncomfortably rapid.

"My teacher and I were greeted by the elder and spent some days exchanging information and preparing for the occasion of the honey hunt. During this time, it became apparent that something was quite wrong with the relationship between the elder and his apprentice. Finally, the elder confided in us that his apprentice was suckling from the devil's teat; he had been seduced into sorcery and the elder had received omens that tragedy might befall the young lad if he did not renounce these ways.

"According to the elder, and in keeping with what *the Bee Master knows*, a temptation toward the dank, stinking tunnel of sorcery occurs at least once in the life of every practitioner of Bee Wisdom. The elder felt that the time of the honey hunt— the most important part of the ceremonial cycle—was the moment of make or break for this young lad. The atmosphere was magnetically black, seductive, and sludgelike around the apprentice, who was about my age then, and about your age now, Twig. Power was moving through him, that much was clear, but a power that did not," whispered Bridge, "answer to our solar jurisdiction."

Bridge continued with his story of how the day arrived for

the hunt to begin and, in due course, the tree containing the bees' nests was found. It was a massive Leguminosae tree, and directly below it was a sacred natural pool, considered to be a gateway to chthonic realms. In Sumatra, only the most experienced shamans had sufficient knowledge of the spirit world to cope with the spiritual and physical dangers of actually collecting the honey. They had to propitiate the spirit of the tree— where the wild hive is found, and whose territory would be invaded if and when the honey was taken. Physical dangers could include encounters with tigers and other wild animals near the tree, falling to one's death while climbing, being stung by a large number of bees, and being poisoned by the tree's sap. The honey collecting was usually done by two shamans, the elder Bee Master acting as the spiritual director and the younger apprentice undertaking the physical work of climbing and collecting the combs.

"The young apprentice climbed the tree carrying a slow-burning torch, singing continuously to induce the bees to leave their comb and follow the red embers that were floating down to the earth, due to the apprentice repeatedly striking the torch against the branch supporting the nest. No metal was allowed to be used. The tools had to be of wood, bamboo, or cane; metal would have offended the spirit of the tree.

"I had been invited to make the climb, too, and we had both fasted for six days and nights. Other spiritual precautions were also taken: There must have been no recent deaths and no family member should be with child."

Both apprentices began the climb, the Kelt and the Asian. Bridge was young and fit, but the apprentice was skilled in the art of tree climbing and went ahead, carrying the torch.

"What happened next was remarkable and awful. Instead of recognizing the young apprentice and working with him, the bees—which are much larger than European bees*—began to attack him mercilessly, stinging him repeatedly until, crying out in agony, he let go of his grip and fell past me screaming, directly into the pool beneath us.

"As he entered the pool, a terrifying and blood-curdling sound came from the depths of the waters. The three of us—my teacher, myself, and the master shaman—saw a grotesque and terrifying creature, identified by the master shaman as a horned water serpent, grab the lad and pull him under. Every act finds its perpetrator, Twig—and despite attempts to trawl the pool, he was never found, and it was accepted that the underworld had taken him. Retribution for betraying the sweet path of the bee priesthood."

Bridge went silent but continued to stare at me. What was he implying? Was I to be tempted on this night by the dark side of the island?

"Remove your clothes, lad; I want you peeled as bare as a willow wand. You need to be naked. Life is naked and the naked body is the truest symbol of life." I was half expecting this command at some point but not at this moment, for I felt there was much more

---

* They would undoubtedly have been the giant bee *Apis dorsata*, which can be the size of small mice.

to be spoken about. As I removed my clothing, Bridge piled the fire high with logs, and as the flames grew, so, too, did the heat. My buttocks, the backs of my legs, and my back were cold, and Bridge continued to talk while I turned before the fire in an attempt to keep warm. It worked only half well and I felt a chill arriving at my anxious heart.

Bridge opened the larger jar and a honeyed scent arrived at my nostrils. He put his hand into the jar, which from what I could see in the half-light contained a white, creamy honey. He approached me, telling me to turn around so I had my back to him. As I did so, I noticed that there was a figure standing directly ahead of me in the shadows, now walking toward me. It was the Bee Mistress, and behind her stood Vivienne, whom I had not seen since our ceremonial encounter. She wore her veil, but I could tell it was she, and as she came forward I could see the outline of her face from the light of the fire. She smiled for a moment as our eyes met, hers ablaze with power. Both then raised their skirts, momentarily displaying their womanhood— no undergarments were worn—this being a symbolic gesture to disperse unbalanced influences within the immediate vicinity.*

The Bee Mistress nodded Vivienne forward, and it was clear she had been instructed as to her duty. Without taking her eyes off me, she dipped her hand into the jar that Bridge was extending to

---

* The Bee Mistress and her charges also urinated standing up, whenever this was practicable. This practice is common in other cultures—Tamil Nadu, southern India, for example.

her and they both began to cover me with honey—Vivienne starting with my forehead and moving down the front of my body, while Bridge began with my feet and moved up its back. I felt absurdly self-conscious and I suddenly thought that this initiation seemed like an act of insanity on my part. I also knew that by casting off my clothes and having the honey smeared onto my body, I had symbolically died. If I were to survive what followed, like the island itself, I would be reborn.

The honey from the larger jar was rubbed into much of my body, but the small of my back, my face, ears, and armpits—where a small nick was made on either side—received only Dark Flight, which Bridge carefully applied. I was then told to scrape out and eat what was left of this mysterious substance within the jar. It amounted to just under two tablespoons of honey, which almost immediately made my mouth tingle and then go numb.

Vivienne's hands reached my genitals and commandingly applied the sticky fluid to my phallus. My eyes caught hers as she looked up and whispered provocatively with a triumphant grin, "You will ride your broomstick tonight, emissary!"

In years to come I would learn that Vivienne was monstrously funny, with perhaps the most astringent sense of humor and gift of mimicry that I have ever encountered. But now, the vision of myself standing naked, covered in a sticky toxic substance that was essentially still a typical household consumable, in cold winds, on a small abandoned island off a densely populated holiday resort, struck me as deeply absurd, and I stifled a laugh. But I was also quite terrified of what lay ahead. *Well, Twig, you wanted adventure, and now you are having it,* I said to myself. As my body became fully covered in a protective shell of honey, I felt warmer against the biting wind and my body temperature began to rise. Soon I was impervious to the roaring winds around me, standing naked and glistening. The Bee Mistress came forward with my Ancestral Rick, tying it around my waste so it hung like a tail from the small of my back, down across my buttocks. Vivienne then handed her one pouch after another, five in all, each one containing pollen, which she sprinkled over my head. She then blew a pinch of it into my face, repeating with each offering the words *nepastovus zmogus*—"changing man"—followed by a simple blessing of the gods: *sudi-u.*

The women took several paces back and began to chant in unison.

Aiii Daiii Idem Jano
Vornio Poroi-ii
Aiiii Daiii Idem Jano
Vornio Poroi-ii . . .

It became a curious, circular, droning Orphic sound, with long, unlikely tones in a language long lost to humans, a vocal narcotic that had me swaying where I stood as I stared into the flames of the fire. As the melody grew gradually more articulate, it seemed so old, so perennial that it was both comforting and disarming. It called to something more archaic than the musical ear, something deeper than taste or reason. The melody seized an inexpressible mood, a noetic vision of the island's dual soul.

Bridge stepped forward so that our eyes met, looking at me as a father might look upon a son going to battle, with tenderness, compassion, and perhaps a note of regret. He began to speak softly, the sound of the women a hypnotic, bewitching backdrop to his words. "I want to give you your instructions for the night, the most important of which is this: Do not fall asleep here, for sleep is the weapon used by the Nightshade Isle. The slightest of accidents can open up sealed, atavistic worlds, and I don't want you getting lost tonight. And do not forget what my story holds for you."

He then began a list of detailed instructions, which he insisted I repeat back to him to ensure that I had fully understood. Now that the Dark Flight had been rubbed onto my skin, there would be two stages to the experience. The first would be a period of contentment and sensitivity, which would be followed by a period of great calm and sluggishness, with a shift in attention from external stimuli to introspection. Sounds would seem to pass by and break up into various other sounds. Spatial awareness would be largely lost and perceived distortions of the body would occur. I might also experience fever, convulsions, and loss of short-term memory. But none of these things must be allowed to distract me from my task—which was to dance to the fire. What lay beyond that, Bridge added, was my fruit to pick. "But pick wisely, Twig. And hesitate, even briefly, and the moment you are here to meet will be lost."

"Dance!" shouted Bridge suddenly. "To the fire and back!" As he said this, he began to play his tanging quoit, which sang with the music of the bees across the landscape. The women increased their singing, and it dashed on in fierce intensity.

As I began to dance, I found that I became erect, though this was quite against my will. Dancing with an erection, I quickly discovered, was extremely uncomfortable, but I was not even momentarily embarrassed, and there was nothing I could have done about it in any case. It was clear to me that this was the work of the Dark Flight, and, remembering the words of the Melissa that I would be riding my broomstick tonight, I grabbed my erection with both hands and continued the dance.

I moved, semi-stumbling, back and forth toward the fire, aware of the stars above that twinkled like glittering fish. I could feel something sweeping down upon me like some fierce storm scattering everything to the winds. To my vision, my erection began to extend itself to an absurd length, some two feet in reach, and it had changed from flesh and blood to what felt and looked like solid wood. I was riding the broomstick, with the Ancestral Rick flailing behind me like a tail or the twigs of a broom, and with every cycle of movement toward the fire and away again, my lurching movements grew gradually more fluid as my body found its own new rhythm.

I was having to hold my attention with the utmost concentration, for if I relaxed, even for a moment, my mind began to ebb away on the currents of some great dark sea, through which my body now seemed to be swimming. My body ebbed and flowed to the roaring fire. My eyes blinkered to the road ahead. It should have been a simple task: Move toward the fire, retreat from the fire, move toward the fire, retreat—yet the effort required was like walking a tightrope over some vast abyss, demanding absolute and dedicated focus on the task. I dared to glance around for just a moment and saw that every face was tense with emotion. I hardly recognized Bridge and it seemed that Vivienne had been transformed—now shaking wildly as a maenad, her blue and yellow dress giving her a curious, snakelike appearance, and her whole body quivering as if she were possessed by the serpent-power itself. I felt as if I were material to be fused in the crucible of the Lord of the Dance, a dance of temperament and force gathered from its own momentum.

The entire area of my genitals began to change once again. The scrotal circumference grew and I let out a cry of pain as I felt skin and sinew expand, stretch, and grow. But the sound I heard released from my throat was not the voice I knew, a human male voice expressing stress and alarm, but rather that of a beast, a stag—*the* stag, he whom I had slain with pollen, whose scrotum I had ritually removed and placed within my Ancestral Rick. I was that stag, merged, symbiotic, its spirit fused with my own—a stag at the peak of my rut, with the magnificent curvature of my rod-shaped penis pointing to the stars. I took in with primal, unblinking eyes my shuddering body as it released a great spray of urine upward into the air. I roared my horned dominance.

Cernunnos, Horned One
Cernunnos, Lord of the Sun,
Herne the hunter and hunted
Stag god of the Earth . . .

Bridge's voice moved in tandem with the women and his quoit. He chanted to the horned one, to the stag god, to Pan, god of the bees, to Herne, to the seed of thrusting primordial life, the women wrapping his chant in a firm ouroboric mantle of dream sound. I saw Bridge standing, facing me from perhaps twenty feet away, holding a crossbow in one hand. He moved slowly, raising it to his eye. But this meant nothing to me, and I continued to dance. My swaying fury and the torrential music abolished all thought, the music that had awakened the sleeping Dionysiac spirit.

. . . the hunter and the hunted . . .

With each step I felt myself change, extending my move-ments further, longer, higher. My body was now moving itself, far beyond my will. I watched, an observer, as I jumped over the flames of the fire, an action theoretically impossible, the orange roar being some six feet across and twice that in height. Yet I seemed to move across and through it with ease. I landed, turned, and began once again to run toward the flames. This time I leapt higher still, and I took off and landed a meter or so beyond the circle of the flames. I landed with grace and ease,

173

breathing in the night air as a powerful and proud stag, snorting and calling—but to what?

The hunter held the crossbow against his shoulder, aiming it at the stag, bellowing at the fire and the stars in virile intensity. Again the stag turned to the fire and I knew this would be my final jump, that some crucial but obscure moment had arrived. I turned and felt the power of life pour through me. If I were to die at this moment, I would die having undertaken my final dance, my final battle, with everything I possessed—as a total act to honor the mystery that was my life.

I was pumping muscle, blood, and manhood as I ran and then lunged, and at that moment I saw an arrow of lightning move toward me. But rather than seeking height and length this time, I jumped low, to receive a baptism from the flames. I jumped into the very heart of the fire as the arrow met my heart. And then all of time stood still.

I heard a voice through the colossal darkness that draped me like a shroud. I was freezing cold, lost in a moment frozen for all eternity. There was nothing around me and no one else was near. Was I sleeping? I heard the voice again, skittering sound patterns that coalesced and disintegrated around me: "Do not fall asleep." But sleep was all I wanted. I felt colder with every moment I spent in this chaos.

A single snowflake fell into the fire, and, distantly, I recognized that it was I within the flames, melting, terrified, and helpless.

Something drifted toward me. A spark? An ember? A flake of snow? No. As it approached, I saw it was a single bee, which entered the fire and found its way onto my hand. It moved up my body and over my lips to the center of my forehead, between my eyes, and then it stung me. I watched this all in slow motion, as if from a distance, as if I were watching a film of me as snow, flesh, fire. I felt the sacred venom enter my bloodstream and watched as the bee moved around in a spiral pattern to remove her stinger without losing her life.

Having met her task, she disappeared through the wall of flame and another bee appeared, this time with six others. They arrived on my neck, and again stung me with their venom. The seventh placed its sting into the top of my head, at the dream wheel. I screamed soundlessly.

There was a moment's pause . . . and then I saw them. Bees emerged from all around me, not from the flames, but from the crater holding the fire, the caldera, the center of the mystery. They arrived in their thousands and moved up my body like a living blanket, covering me in entirety. I felt their feet move across my skin, and they began to lick the honey from me. This time, there was no pain—only ecstasy.

I saw their sound, like light waves colliding off my body, their collective hum beginning to make sense. I heard words, saw pictures, and experienced emotions all together, as one single unit of information from the hive, and I knew this was the Song of the Bee, and the words must be remembered. But I was so tired. Every time I began to slip into the arms of sleep, rocked into the gentle night by the lullaby of the bees, there was a sharp and distinct pain as a stinger released its venom into my body, and the song continued. It was the song of creation.

The Eternal Parent was wrapped in the sleep of Cosmic Night
Light there was not, for the Flame of Spirit had not yet been rekindled.
Time there was not, for change had not yet re-begun
Things there were not, for form had not yet re-presented itself, neither
was there action for there were no manifested things to act.
There being no things, there were no opposites to manifest and thus no
polarity.
But this Eternal Parent, causeless, indivisible, changeless, and Infinite,
rested in unconscious dreamless sleep, and other than this Eternal
Parent there was naught, either real or apparent.
The germ within the Cosmic egg takes unto itself form.
The Flame is rekindled.
Time begins and Things exist, and with these changes, action and
polarities spring into being and the cosmos makes love to itself
and the genesis of a World Soul comes into manifestation.
Thus the One becomes the Two, the neuter becomes bisexual, male and
female, the two in one are evolved from the neuter, and generation begins.
The One becoming two generates the many, thus the Unity becomes
diversity, the identical becomes variety yet the many remain the
One.
Diversity remains Unity and variety remains identical. Thus while
there is variation of manifestation, the essentiality of the One
remains.

The One is the Flame of Life; the many are the Sparks of the Flame.
Thus life is the essence of the Spirit and consciousness is the essence of
Life. Spirit is One, an essential Unity manifesting in diverse forms
of life, which life is itself as One manifesting in diverse forms of
consciousness.
Thus from a Creator, the Creation is manifested.

This story of creation continued to unfold, accompanied by detailed images moving through the history of the cosmos, and then our universe, and then our solar system, and eventually our Earth, our home. I saw tectonic plates migrate slowly across Earth, interacting with each other in complex ways: some rubbing against their neighbors, others colliding head-on, and still others slipping beneath adjacent ones to melt back into the depths below like the disappearing end of a conveyor belt until they rose again as new molten matter rises up from below mid-ocean rifts to cool and solidify into rock. Earth was ever moving; mountains rose, rocks were ground down, oceans were widened, and continents were realigned—all as a result of slow, tectonic migrations across the face of the molten globe. But beyond that, the world was empty and silent, waiting for the diversity of life to arrive.

Time moved on and then they came; I witnessed what Adam had seen on the morning of his creation—the miracle, moment by moment, of naked existence. From infinity itself they came; the great swarm of spiraling lemniscates arrived, carrying the genetic codes and blueprints for all of life on Earth, the patterns of inheritance. The winged cosmic helix spirals arrived and plunged deep into the earth, bringing myths in their movement, each one a singing, vibrating string; creative magic expressed itself in a symphony of divine harmonies. The intertidal shellfish rose and flower-headed zoophytes from a strange age of naked, plantless lands evolved around the sweeping fishless seas that had no names. Within and beneath this incomprehensible, predestined march of a million summers and faded pictures, the fish, our ancestors, rushed through the waters of later worlds. The first bees, flying over colossal forests whose feet stood in slime, living in pairs and small families, evaded the great spiders and centipedes. Dragonflies with two-foot wings nested in the undergrowth at the edge of a limitless sea. Continents started to separate. Relationships between the first honeybees and our human ancestors began. The Path of Pollen was born upon the Nightshade Isle.

Generation after generation of women and men within the cultus were shown to me—their faces, temperaments, strengths, gifts, and tasks—and I saw each one as they were inducted into the Way of the Bee. Finally, I recognized the face of young Bridge as he underwent his own initiation into the hive.

And then it left, this great flow of information, like bees taking flight or the smoke of a fire spiraling upward into the distant clouds. I arrived back in the present and, in image and reality, I became aware of the first light. I was knowingly human once again, back in the miraculous illusion of stability we have learned to call reality.

The flames had receded, and only one or two bees remained on my skin, licking the final small drops of honey from me.

The fire had been replaced by a smoldering ash, and the once raging heat was now just a warm glow beneath me, my Ancestral Rick still, remarkably, tied to my waist and only a little charred. I looked up and saw Bridge sitting by his satchel. He nodded gently and smiled. The Bee Mistress was gone, as was Vivienne. *How remarkable to be a human being*, I thought.

I stood up and the bees flew back to their hives. I knew that my first responsibility was to thank the bees and tell them my vision and my words. I moved to the first hive and began to relay my story. They softly murmured in approval and I moved to the next hive, and on to the next, until I had traveled the circle and shared everything fully. Then I went back to the smoldering ashes held within the navel of our world.

Bridge had gathered my clothes and his belongings and we began to walk back to the boat in silence, I walking naked in the early-morning light, the few clouds glowing like coals fresh from a fire. I went down to the wine-colored sea, where a soft morning mist greeted me, and I watched the streaks of first sunlight, which Bridge spoke of as the Golden Arrows of Dawn. For a moment I sat, looking down at the faint light on the water and feeling the ash in my hair and between my toes, and then I hit the waves with a dive that stung my belly as I plunged into the water's icy embrace. I then rose from the sea's lustration as if reborn. Indeed, like the island itself, I had been born again—born first of the womb and now of the rite—and I knew the island could have claimed me in this second birth.

The two women were waiting by the small boat as we clambered in. I was suddenly exhausted. The Bee Mistress produced a flask of steaming sweet cherry soup, a favorite recipe from the land of her ancestors, and Bridge passed around a bar of Kendal Mint Cake. After I ate, I was allowed to sleep, and I dreamt I was a baby, swathed in a soft white blanket, being gently held and lovingly whispered to in the arms of my mother. The sound of Bridge singing his homeward song came and went as we headed back to English soil upon the long and even swells.

> *Harvest home, harvest home,*
> *We've plowed, we've sowed,*
> *We've reaped, we've mowed.*
> *And brought safe home every load.*

9

Earth's Embrace

> . . . let honey
> overflow in
> infinite
> tongues,
> and let the ocean become
> a hive . . .
>
> PABLO NERUDA,
> "ODE TO THE BEE"

It took me by surprise when Bridge told me it was time for us to make a further journey. This time we would go not across the waves, but over the land and down to a part of Britain that was almost as beloved by Bridge as Wales, his homeland. We were to be heading for Kernow, or Cornwall, specifically the area of West Penwith, a few square miles in the extreme southwest of Britain. Truly it is the end of the land. Before departing in the relative comfort of the car to travel on tarmac and concrete roads, Bridge indicated that we should also be arriving there on other roads—those of an entirely different substance.

"The Bee Master knows there are three roads leading to Kernow, young Twig: the public, the private, and the secret. We can approach it by the public high road of history, which leads through a rich country; its influence twines like a golden thread through the story of our islands. Or we can come to Kernow by the private upland path of legend. In and out weave the ancient folk stories, full of significance to those whose hearts are attuned to their key. And there is still a third way to arrive at this place: the secret Green Road of the soul that leads through the hidden door into a land known only to the Strong Eye, the eye of vision.

"Kernow has an attraction for us, bearing as it does traces of those sunken islands, Lyonesse and Atlantis, which are lost in the depth of our minds. This place has always exerted a magnetic pull; we are irresistibly drawn here to undertake certain work." Little did I know he was uttering prophetic words, for the impact of the work I was to do here would in time impel me to make this landscape my home.

A wide sky stretched ahead of us as we began the long drive. Our familiar cloth of silence fell upon us, our habit, and within this monastic stillness much moved—no awkwardness here, but authentic active silence.

In due time Bridge spoke, setting in motion a certain tone, without yet revealing the exact nature of the work that lay ahead: *"The Bee Master knows* the life of any region depends ultimately on its geologic substratum, for this sets up a chain reaction that passes through the land's streams and wells, its vegetation and the animal life that feeds on this, and finally through the type of human being attracted to live there. In a profound sense, the structure of the land's rocks gives rise to its inner life. Granite, serpentine, slate, sandstone, limestone, chalk—all have their special personality dependent on the age in which they were laid down, each being tied to a special phase of the earth's destiny. The substratum is the collective equivalent of the repressed unconsciouness in the individual. It is the dreamlife and the dreamtime of phantasm and myth. It is also the shadow realm. So, Twig, it all begins beneath the surface of the earth." Continuing without so much as a pause, he began to relate one of Grimm's fairy tales, the story of an obstinate child. As shocking as the story was the fact that he related it in perfect German, a language I spoke with some fluency but that I had no idea he spoke. He named the story "Das Eigensinnige Kind," The Child with Its Own Mind.

"There was a child who would not do what his mother wanted, so in the end God had no goodwill toward it, and it died," Bridge began. "When it was buried, it kept pushing its arm up through the soil—that is, until its mother came and knocked down its arm with a stick. After that, it was for the first time peaceful under the soil, within the arms of its True Mother, the earth."

And that was the whole tale. I knew that it was being told to me not as a warning to naughty infants—it was rather too late for this—but as a glimpse of the dark side of the nature of things. "So you see, Twig, it all begins beneath the surface of the earth," he said again. And as the landscape changed beyond my window from rolling hills to an unforgiving wildness, I reflected on how the old tales offer a far greater bounty than those of contemporary social realism.

It took most of the day and into the early evening before we saw Land's End Peninsula, with its distant, dark blue, brooding hills. The journey was nearly complete, and we began to move along small lanes with sharp turns, clearly having been constructed with the horse-drawn wagon rather than the horseless carriage in mind. Eventually we pulled up at a small, isolated farmhouse bed-and-breakfast that lay beside the moors. The proprietress came out to welcome us. She was an attractive woman of Scandinavian coloring with a compact body, eyes the color of horn, and white-blond hair wound in plaits. She looked me up and down and then said something to Bridge in a language I did not understand, so I asked Bridge what it was.

"I was speaking to your uncle in Cornish," she replied firmly as she wiped her hands on her red-checked apron and narrowed her eyes at me. Her comment seemed to delight and amuse Bridge; clearly they knew each other. I spied several beehives tucked away behind a sheltered wall.

After being shown to our rooms, we went downstairs to a small room with a dark pink carpet that served as a dining area, where our hostess was pouring coal onto the grate. As the coals hissed, we were served a meal of steaming Cornish broth and tea dispensed from a large silver pot. Our meal concluded, we left the house. I did not have to be told where we were headed.

We passed through the garden, the light from the kitchen ribboned out upon it. It seemed so neat and orderly that it was as if a strip of Holland had been transported to Cornwall. There was a balsamic quality in the air and the molecular dance of the particles composing a darkened sky could be felt. Around the stone wall stood our destination: the hives. And around them were flaunted the sweet-smelling pink tassels of dracaenas, or dragon trees, and the leaves of the *Gunnera*, a plant imported from South America that sometimes spread to a span of six feet, hiding in hollows, red-toothed like a ferocious rhubarb, with sticky cones of bloom. But it was the clumps of bamboo, smelling of damp Eastern fabrics from a trunk just opened, that even now reminds me of my time in Kernow with Bridge.

The Bee Master went to each of the three hives and began to hum, croon, and sing as I had witnessed countless times before. I never lost my fascination in watching the bees emerge and alight upon him. He quietly told the bees of our work— which had yet to be revealed to me—and listened to the hive wisdom held in their hum. I, too, undertook my communion with the hives, and yes, they came and alighted upon me, too. Although I noted that their dance and song were perhaps less eagerly affectionate than those shared with the Bee Master, they nevertheless arrived to hear my words and to talk in honeyed tongues. This task undertaken, a line was drawn in the sand under the day. It was time to rest.

The next morning we set off early by foot, but not before Bridge requested that I bring his satchel and a shovel from the

back of his aged Ford Zephyr. The rain, which had started to fall
during the night, had not let up, and the wild wind bullied us on
our walk across the moors. As we continued, Bridge commented
that this part of Britain needed to be walked, strolled over, and
scaled many times before it could be properly known. "Observe,
Twig: The character of this place is small in scale; there are no
great heights or depths and, except for the coast, it is hardly
spectacular. But it is an enchanted place. A breath of peace
arrives through a drift of furze bloom; a carvedstone cross at the
fork of a road indicates tracings of the sacred. Twig, the landscape is intensely varied and can change completely in the space
of a few paces; and it is for this reason that those who tear
through it miss most of its beauty. This was the landscape that
felt the tread of human feet over five thousand years ago, called
here as we are called today."

His words caused me to examine my surroundings with
greater vigilance. The detail he spoke of revealed itself in
the complexity of plant life around me. Startling yellow gorse,
the neighbor to wild sorrel and garlic, was a gamut of nourishment at my feet.

We walked on through the morning, a blue-gray Cornish
morning, stopping for a ploughman's lunch at a lonely pub. Later
we arrived at a narrow lane that meandered on and on, the surface growing ever poorer, the air more lonely, until there was no
more than a barren track to walk. The rain had finally ceased
and the sun was now firmly on our backs. Eventually a mead-
owed hillock stood before us, crowned with scattered boulders

of granite and rocks of immense size, cloaked with exotic heaths and azaleas. We walked around it and I noticed a spring oozing from beneath a rock, making a muddy puddle that spilled into the undergrowth. There was a tantalizing air of enchantment about the unspectacular fading foliage.

Bridge suddenly pulled at me sharply and we left the track, entering what appeared to be a green tunnel, overhung with rich, dark, subtropical vegetation, boughs growing from either side and greeting each other overhead. This verdant tunnel unfurled ahead of us and led to the entrance of a hidden stone passage. Bridge parted the curtain of ivy and brambles that covered its entrance and we crept through its opening. We moved along the well-constructed passage that in turn led to a circular, corbeled chamber. It was like the inside of an underground tower. The air was warmer here and the depth of peace that enfolded the spot could not be explained by the vegetation and granite alone. I felt as if the top of my head had been painlessly sliced off and no longer existed. A penumbral light slid down its damp walls, filtered by green tendrils that partially concealed a small roof, opening to the outside, and showed spikes of navelwort growing from the crannies of the stones. Bridge lovingly touched the walls as if he were greeting an old friend. Until now he had not said a word, which had exacerbated my anxiety. Finally, he began to speak.

"*The Bee Master knows* this place as the Beehive Hut. It is the antechamber to receiving the earth's embrace."

His voice was characterized by a rich and resonant quality

and I could see why the chamber had been so named, for it looked akin to the inner structure of a bee skep but was completely subterranean. It held a certain charged atmosphere.

As explanation for the elegant sound, Bridge remarked, "This specific ritual environment was created in recognition of the particular acoustical properties it could create. We sing to the bees when ceremony is being undertaken, but the ceremony is not done by the person within the Beehive Hut, but rather by the person who is also subterranean, who carries a yet closer communion with the earth.

"Our True Mother the Earth has extraordinary patience for her children. After all, she births everything in order that all experiences may be had. But her patience does have its limits. Sometimes she cleanses herself through what we call natural catastrophes such as earthquakes, volcanic eruptions, radical weather conditions, and so forth. These are the rumblings of an upset gut, the straining and flexing of tired muscles, the renewals and revitalizations of her body. In the modern world, this has been forgotten; modern man and woman no longer feel and know Earth as a whole living being, as a teacher, as our Mother. On this night, you will be returned to her again—to the source of life—and you will also be with the Changer."

"The Changer?" I asked, feeling the snake of unrest moving in my stomach.

"*The Bee Master knows* death as the Changer and she will visit you on this night as well. It is a night of being wrapped within life and confronted by death. *The Bee Master knows* that of all the ceremonies the apprentice is put through within the Path of Pollen, this one is without doubt the most primal, and without doubt mirrors our most primal fear. It is the ceremony of being buried alive, being buried within Earth to receive her embrace. We undertake this ceremony for the following reasons. First, *the Bee Master knows* that the earth is the ultimate source of everything we are, and in aspiration to meet the first Bee Master—the Sorcerer—we return to this source, allowing the sorcerer within us to evolve and be instructed. Second, the work on this path demands that we hold a strong anchoring to the earth. If this anchor is not firmly in place, the flight of the Bee—our flight—can become as the final flight of Icarus; we may rise too closely to the sun and, like Icarus's, our wings may melt away. Superstition, madness, and death lie there, and such is the plight of many a light chaser. We upon the Path of Pollen know that with every step of ascent toward light, there must be an equal and opposite descent into darkness; the shadow of nature is that which is undisclosed and to be discovered. This is why burial is common at death—as the opportunity to come to the knowledge of the iridescence-below-ground in the clear state of the soul's awakening at death. But upon this path we do not wait until death takes us to seek this knowledge. We give ourselves to death in advance."

The idea of being buried alive sounded insane, but at this stage I had no idea if he was being literal, although I had learned that there was usually a very physical and literal aspect to his teachings.

It was time to start with the preparations and I was told to lie down on a flat patch of earth near the entrance to the Beehive Hut. I lay down on the cool, damp ground, and the Bee Master made an outline of my body with bright orange and yellow pollen. I then got up and saw what looked like the shape of an Egyptian sarcophagus upon the bright green grass. He handed the shovel to me, indicating that it was time to begin my dig, and I began to cut up the sod by pushing the spade horizontally under the grass to loosen it and then peel it away from the soil and place it above the grave. I continued to do this until the area was clear of grass, so that there was a positive and negative image of my shape. Before Bridge went to collect wood for the fire that would be keeping him company through the night, he instructed me to continue digging my grave.

I watched the shovel make its cut as my foot forced it down into the black, my arms then levering it up and out of my growing tomb. My body was fully engaged but my mind sought hibernation against a thudding inquisition forming within. "To *dig* one's own grave. To dig one's *own* grave." This statement was becoming wallpaper over all other thought. *Tonight I might die—* heart attack, seizure, suffocation—but my location could not be more appropriate. I would at least be in the right place. Bridge maintained that life should be lived as if each day was one's last, the point being that one day this will be the case. *And it might be tonight. How perfect if I were to die in a grave of my own making.*

The weather had moved once again; it was now gray and chilly, and a faint mist that had stood a distance away was moving and threatened to cover me. During the whole of a dull, dark, and soundless day, I reflected on the entombment that lay ahead until the grave was some four feet deep. There was a huge mound of earth next to the grave, the light was going, and I was sure I was done.

Bridge returned on and off with piles of fallen wood, simply muttering "Not deep enough" before disappearing again. He finally reappeared with food and went back to his work; I saw him place offerings of pollen at various parts of the site. And then he returned and spoke: "Enough, Twig—your grave is ready for you."

The Bee Master unfolded a long, narrow bundle from his satchel, which held the two femur bones from the stag that I had hunted and killed. They had been hollowed and worked so that they were now attached to each other, appearing like the leg from some unnamed creature who resided in the shadow lands I was soon to visit. "This will be your snorkel as you dive deeply into the arms of your Mother. Remember: The nearer the bone, the sweeter the flesh," Bridge said, holding the bone to his lips and breathing through it. He passed it to me and I held it to my lips, noting that one end had been cushioned in beeswax so that the bone would not cut into the lips or gums. He got the fire going and bade me sit as he spoke his words of advice for the ceremony ahead.

"*The Bee Master knows* that Earth waits for you; she waits patiently and longs to give you her embrace, an embrace that is a holding like none other is able to offer you. Tonight you will be reunited with your True Mother, she who has given you your life—our lives—all life here around us. When you are buried, you will speak to her of your hopes and your dreams, your regrets and your sorrows, your wants and your needs. She understands you, for she is your Mother. She can bring you what you need, for all she wants is for her son to meet all the appointments he has been born to meet. You have an opportunity tonight to literally bury anything of your past that no longer serves you; ask your Mother to take it so that you can step more fully into the tasks you have come to undertake."

I nodded in understanding. In these few words, much of my fear had been removed.

"But Twig, I also wish you to call out to the Changer, to death herself—the Great Huntress. I want you to ask her what you can learn from her. Do not be alarmed by calling to the Changer; it will not hasten the final appointment you have on Earth, the appointment you have with her when you leave our Earth. Rarely do people ask death for advice regarding life, but whom better to ask? Who can know more regarding life than the Changer? There is no greater informant than she who ultimately extinguishes all animation. This is not a night for sleep, but a night for meeting your appointments with both she who gave you your life and she who will at some moment come for it."

Bridge concluded his talk by asking if I had any queries—I did not—and by telling me that he would be by the side of the fire or within the Beehive Hut through the night. This gave me some comfort, but he added that it was unlikely he would hear me if I called out.

Bridge then took a wad of beeswax out of his pocket and told me to stuff my ears and nostrils with the wax and, once done, to step into the grave. Ahead of me he threw a handful of pollen into the tomb.

I looked down into my grave, which had a yellow glow within it, the light of the fire illuminating the Golden Coins, spilling honey light. I climbed down into my grave and lay upon the pollen-covered earth. A band of moonlight slowly crept on one side of the grave, revealing the layering of soil, each telling a story from the age of its formation.

Bridge began to shovel the soil on top of me from the great mound I had spent the day piling up. Initially the sensation was not threatening—more intriguing, reminding me of times as a child at the beach when I would cover myself in sand. I remembered struggling free from the weight of the sand when I had been buried by my brother. But once the first layer of soil had arrived over all of my body except my head—which Bridge left open to the air—the fascination of this new sensation left me and was replaced by a weight—the weight of the soil, which was considerable. Bridge then came to my head and indicated that I release the hand that was holding the bone to my lips. Then, as if he was going to perform a conjuring trick, he showed me two coins; but I knew what he intended with them. Just as the ancient Greeks placed coins on the eyelids of the dead as payment to the boatman on the river Styx for ferrying the dead to the other side, here was a symbolic payment to the Earth so that I could see in the darkness with the Strong Eye and witness all that came during my night. I could feel my forehead crease as I clamped my eyes shut. Bridge put his fingers gently on my eyelids and then placed the coins upon them. He held the bone erect and began to scoop soil, first gently placing the soil on my face and then, once my face was covered, scooping it in large measure, the weight of the soil growing by the moment, the bone now held in place at my lips by the soil around it.

And then utter silence arrived. Within this silence, I felt the weight of earth against me gradually increase as Bridge continued to pile up the soil upon my covered body. My breathing bone worked well, but I wondered what would happen if it broke in the night, letting cold soil pour into my mouth, causing me to breathe in solid earth, drowning in that which had given me life. The weight of silence, weight of earth.

I had descended into the cellar without a candle. There was nothing except the sound of my breathing in and out. I could not move; there was no doubt that even if I wanted to, I could not escape this place.

I had no choice but to lie still. The layers above me were lead-heavy. I wondered what influences, essences, presences would arrive on this night. A roar, deep in tone and musical, began swelling up around me. It felt like a wind, but how could it be? It was a muffled clamor that seemed to recede when I placed my attention on it. For a moment, I thought it was the sound of Bridge's car and that he was deserting me, driving away. Or was it somehow the sound of the sea grinding the immense boulders not half a mile from here? No, it was the sound of my body, my blood moving through the arteries and veins, my muscles adjusting and readjusting to the weight upon them, and my bones following them, shifting, cartilage and ligament working against the downward force. Every sound from every part of my body was audible. I was drowning in noise.

As instructed, I began to talk silently to the one who gave me life—swathed in her blanket, wrapped in her mantle—and as I did so, I felt myself falling backward and down like a sky diver. I was falling ever deeper and farther into the arms of my Mother, free-falling with no fear toward a warmth that stemmed from the deeply banked furnace fires within her depths. It was the solar womb of the Earth I was dropping into, with the dream of being born anew. It was luxurious and welcoming, rich. I fell into the place between sleep and waking, the betwixt and between place, and I saw myself rise out of the Earth and join the Bee Master by the fire. He was singing and playing the quoit. He briefly looked in my direction when I arrived and then continued with his singing and playing as I danced to the fire.

I woke up with a start, realizing I must have fallen asleep. For a moment I forgot where I was. Then I saw I was in a small, dark room, and in front of me I could feel a door. I reached for the door handle but could find none. I moved my fingers to the side of the door to feel for hinges; yes, here they were. I tried to make the door open, pushing against it, kicking it, and finally it opened just a crack, just slightly. Something fell on me and I yelled and let go of the door. I picked up what had fallen. It was soft and fell apart in my hands and it smelled familiar. I thought for a moment. *"It's soil. But where, God Almighty, where am I?"* But I knew where I was. I had been buried alive and I was within a casket, a coffin. I began to claw at the interior of it, moving into sheer terror, and then I awoke and began to fall, fall onto the sharpened stakes of a leaf-covered pit, punctured as I held my intestines in my hands, my chest split open like a piece of fruit, nothing but red all around me.

But I awoke from this nightmare into knowing that I was trapped beneath the earth, without the luxury of a lined coffin, my lifeline of a stag bone jutting from my mouth. The womb of the Earth now felt like monster's jaws—a *vagina dentata*. I moved into overwhelming and engulfing fear for my life and I struggled to suck air into my lungs through the bone, which felt as if it had become partially blocked. I could feel the presence of something creeping upon me, by slow yet certain degrees. An irrepressible tremor gradually pervaded my frame; and at length, there sat upon my very heart a succubus—a she-demon. It bore down on me, heavy as the history of all my nightmares, drawing life from me, threatening to leave me withered and useless, a barren husk abandoned in the earth. If this apparition was the Changer, I knew there was no way I could shake it off. I screamed to it: Do not take me, I have so much more to do, so much more to learn. I was full of rage with death and I vented my fury.

The vision receded and I thought I had defeated it. But it was merely the preamble. Growing around me, seeping into all that I was, came the Huntress. The flickering wing of a dove, a sensed silhouette, and an infinite expanse of water, glass still, unmoving, a lake that contains all time; the Silencer of all is here and I am mute in her presence. I felt her wrap me in her dark wings, and in the presence of death I saw my life: how petty I had been in my actions, what a judge I was of others, my arrogance, my indifference, my cynicism, and my pride. I was filled with regrets for wasting so much precious time, for putting off so much to a nonexistent tomorrow.

Then I found my voice. I made pledges to the Changer—promises that I would not waste precious time, that I would make all of the appointments I was born to meet. As I made my pledges, it was as though I moved from the periphery of my being—the body that contained me—to the very center of myself, a place that was imperturbable, totally quiet, and at rest. I lost my shape and became as sperm, returning to a state of pure vitality, semen within the womb of the Earth. And then it happened: The semen began to re-form into human shape, all that no longer served me having been taken by the Earth, and my form arrived anew.

I felt a trickle of water, just a drop, and then another. It was the sweetest water I had ever tasted. It was raining. I could feel each droplet as it entered my mouth and slipped down my throat. The life-giving hollow bone was bringing me water of a new life.

> *Along which secret aqueduct,*
> *Oh water, are you coming to me,*
> *water of a new life*
> *that I have never drunk.*

I lay in the earth, swaddled, knowing that I was alive, a gift of life manifest, clear about my tasks, an emissary-child of the hive and Earth. I began to feel movement above me. It was the Bee Master, the one who had brought me to the door of so many riches.

10

The Kelt Falls

The Kelt falls, but his spirit rises in the heart
and brain of the Anglo-Keltic peoples, with whom
are the destinies of the generations to come.

FIONA MACLEOD

W hat is it, this life?

I know, I *know*, that between the investigations, the calcula-
tions, the quantifications, and the rationalizations of the scientist, there is a gap, like the white space between words or the
pause in a sentence that gives meaning to the spoken word.

Life can be sliced into slithers on a laboratory slide—diagnosed, theorized, hypothesized, enriched, enlivened, denied,
imprisoned, given—and ended. But what is life really? Have any
of our great philosophers, our scientists, our "men of God" ever
really answered the question? Have they even come close to
addressing it?

What is it that gave the flesh on the laboratory slide a purpose and a personality, made it animate, a living thing, with
emotions and meaning and soul?

There is something that endures beyond us, some spirit, some essence, some eternal thing that can never be created in a lab or observed through a microscope. If we ever stop to think about it, every step we take in life is a colossal leap of faith that leaves the rational mind reeling: that we are here at all with a purpose to perform, that we will not cease to exist with the next breath in, that we are walking toward a conclusion of some sort, that the journey itself has meaning. We hurtle through space at thousands of miles a second, human time machines, into a destiny we co-create with the cosmos itself. Time and space and us. Ultimately, it all amounts to the same thing: a simple act of faith.

I *know* all this and I know that, our purpose fulfilled, we will leave this world and return to the pure essence of ourselves. Such partings are the actions of warriors and should be a cause for celebration, a round of applause for a life lived fully, answers found, a truth discovered, a purpose served. But sometimes they are not.

I was at home repairing one of my hives when the phone call came. At first I was too stunned to feel anything. Bridge—my mentor, my teacher, my companion, my friend—was dead. I stumbled into my car and began to drive.

The phone call had come from Morag, who had found Bridge alone in the orchard, surrounded by the hives. As in life, so in death: He had walked out of his body and passed from this world in the company of his beloved bees.

Shortly after having met Bridge, he told me how the bees will sometimes moan as if with pain under certain circumstances. And although I did not dismiss this as a folktale, I had secretly scoffed at the idea, particularly because Bridge had not claimed to have witnessed this phenomenon. But on the occasion of his death, Morag had found the hives emitting a deep, mournful hum, as if the bees themselves were in pain. Bridge was lying next to the hives, as if sleeping.

Still, I would not have believed it had I not witnessed this supernatural phenomenon myself, some three hours of frantic driving later. When I arrived, the bees were still in a state of considerable agitation, emitting the keening of nature herself lamenting the passing of one of her beloved children.

In accordance with tradition, the hives had already been turned 180 degrees and wrapped by the Bee Mistress in bands of black crape. The body was covered in a favorite blanket, stained with the marks of sticky propolis from a dozen or more years of carrying the hives to the Nightshade Isle.

I looked down at my friend's long form beneath the blanket, part of me still expecting him to spring up at any moment— unable to accept, with my heart or my mind, that Bridge was truly dead. He had always seemed so vital, so alive, so immune to death. And there was part of me that knew this was the view of a fool who had fallen for the Western definition of death as a failure of some kind, instead of a sacred moment of ultimate achievement, a purpose fulfilled.

It was as if Earth recognized my need for stability and drew me down to the grass, and I found myself sitting next to Bridge, as serene as Socrates after the hemlock. Between us lay another body, that of a beautiful golden creature that had clearly only moments before stopped breathing. The sight of this one single bee triggered the sorrow of my loss and I burst into tears, the sound of my sobbing echoing that of the bees who wept around me, and I was left alone in the orchard with the hives to weep, to grieve.

The tides of evening came slowly at that time of year, but to me it was suddenly dusk when I finally emerged from my grief hours later. A strange stillness had descended on the orchard and the sound of the hives began to diminish, become a hush, and then a gentle hum.

I looked toward the hives as the sound began to fade—and there stood Bridge. I watched in silence and in awe as his delicate form—his incorporeal shade—moved from hive to hive, saying his farewells and blessing the hives one by one as I had seen him do on countless occasions. And then he turned toward me.

Tears were pouring down my cheeks as his presence before me melted my heart still further, and he laid his hand gently on the top of my head. "You are my pollen," he said simply as he smiled down at me, admonition whispered from teacher to student at the parting of ways. Then the form began to fade, silently becoming more and more opaque, like a morning mist blown by winds as he evanesced to his Elysian fields of heavenly mead and honey.

Someone with a hundred million golden sparkling parts, without which the Earth would have been a poorer and less fruitful place, had gone.

Afterword

The death of Bridge fell heavily upon all those within the community associated with the Path of Pollen. Through his death, I met a number of other remarkable confreres and keepers of hive wisdom, and what I had suspected was finally confirmed to me: that Bridge had been considered the living elder, the Pollen King, of the tradition, and was revered as such. I inherited Bridge's smoker, tanging quoits, hive tools, and the hives themselves, and I went on that year to have the richest crop of honey I have ever had.

I felt compelled to write this book in the hope that it will contribute to the rediscovery of a most remarkable body of knowledge. Books sometimes survive across several generations, and I would like to address these last words to you who may pick up this book a hundred years from now. Whoever you are—perhaps the child of a child of someone I once knew—if the thoughts and teachings contained within this book are real, then they will speak to you across the years with directness and meaning. In that moment of meeting you will know that you are not alone and that we—practitioners of Bee Wisdom—have something worthwhile to offer you.

At the time that I wrote this book, the prophets of doom were constantly telling us that we were about to destroy ourselves with warfare, toxins, and overpopulation. Still, Earth endured. Perhaps the same words are being spoken to you now; but you will know some of the answers.

If the words in this book have touched you, I invite you to deepen your contact with the world of our most ancient ally: the honeybee. Perhaps you can make contact with a local bee-keeper, one of the old-timers who can show you something of what I have written here and can even perhaps guide you toward the Bee Masters and Bee Mistresses who await their aspirants with sweet welcome.

Tá na ródannaí meala ag na beach in ins gach aird den sliabh.

Bibliography

Butler, Charles. *The Feminine Monarchie.* Oxford: Joseph Barnes, 1609.

Campbell, Joseph. *Primitive Mythology.* New York: Penguin Books, 1991.

DeForest. Clinton J. *Folk Medicine,* New York: Fawcett Books, 1985.

Eliade, Mircea. *The Sacred and the Profane.* New York: Harcourt, Brace and World, 1959.

———. *Shamanism: Archaic Techniques of Ecstasy.* Bollingen Series LXXVI. New York: Pantheon, 1964.

Frazer, Sir James G. *The Golden Bough.* New York: Macmillan, 1922.

Gaignebet, C. *Art profane et religion populaire au moyen-âge.* Paris: Presses Universitaires de France, 1985.

Harner, Michael J. *The Way of the Shaman.* New York: HarperCollins, 1990.

———, ed. *Hallucinogens and Shamanism.* New York: Oxford University Press, 1973.

Harner, Sandra, and Warren W. Tryon. *Psychological and Immunological Responses to Shamanic Journeying with Drumming.* Paper presented at the Third International Conference of the International Society for Shamanic Research, Nara, Japan, September 1995.

Kovacs, Attila S. *Folk Culture of the Hungarians.* Budapest: Museum of Ethnography, 1997.

Lucke, H. *Wundbehandlung mit Honig und Lebertran*. Frankfurt: Deutsche Med Wochenschrift, 1935.

Machado, Antonio. *Times Alone*. Middletown, Conn.: Wesleyan University Press, 1983.

Neruda, Pablo N. *Full Woman, Fleshy Apple, Hot Moon*. Translated by Stephen Mitchell. New York: HarperCollins, 1997.

Parra, R., and Jaime Hernando. *Los Cuentos de los Abuelos*. Quito: Ediciones Abya-Yala, 1997.

Pessoa, Fernando. *Obras Completas*. Lisbon: Atica, 1973.

Schultes, Richard E. *Pharmacognosy: The Pharmaceutical Sciences*. Third Lecture Series, Harvard University 19 (1960): 109–22.

Snellgrove, L. E. *Wound Treatment with Honey*. Privately published, Hereford, U.K., 1922.

Schweisheimer, W. "Cancer and Beekeeping." *Gleanings in Bee Culture* 9 (September 1967): 360, 561.

Tylor, Edward B. *Primitive Culture: Researches into the Development of Mythology, Philosophy, Religion, Language, Art and Custom*. 2 vols. 1871.

Uccusic, Paul. *Bee Medicine*. Vienna: Facultas, 1982.

Virgil. *The Georgics*. Translated by L. P. Wilkinson. New York: Viking Press, 1983.

Wier, Jean. *Histoires, disputes et discours*. Vol. 2. 1660. Reprint, Paris: Bureau du Progrès Médical, 1885.

Yeats, William Butler. *Yeats's Poems*. Edited by A. Norman Jeffares. Dublin: Gill and Macmillan, 1989.

BOOKS OF RELATED INTEREST

Inner Traditions • Bear & Company
P.O. Box 388
Rochester, VT 05767
1-800-246-8648
www.InnerTraditions.com
Or contact your local bookseller